The Untold Stories Of Ectopic Pregnancies

by Cindy Sexton

DEDICATION

I dedicate this book to my loving Husband Mike.

Mike you have been my strength and my rock. You have stuck by my side through

all of my emotional roller coasters and I am so blessed to have you in my life.

I love you with all my heart and soul.

SPECIAL THANKS

I want to thank my very special and best friend Kathryn for her inspiration and

always helping me and guiding me. (I know our angels are playing together in

heaven and getting into mischief)

Please take a moment and visit Kathryn's Facebook page Gabby's Cuddles at:

https://www.facebook.com/Gabbyscuddles?ref=br_tf

Also

A special thanks to a very dear friend Alisha for always having sweet words of

encouragement and always helping everyone that she can and also for her Secret

Sister page on Facebook and her Angel Babies page. Please take a moment to visit

her page Angel Babies at:

https://www.facebook.com/pages/Angel-Babies/177888205646436

__Thank you to everyone that contributed stories for this book!! We are all__

__survivors and I hope our stories reach many families in their time of need.__

__We are a family now connected by our babies.__

A few poems that I wrote that are dear to my heart

My Little One
My first gift was your father and then
God gave me you. The emptiness I now
feel inside is too deep to understand. Oh
little one - you see It's very hard for me,
I'll never try to understand why I never
touched your hand or kissed your
forehead. They say there's always a
reason but that doesn't ease my pain.
You've made me cry to say goodbye...To
know I will see you again in Heaven is
a blessing to no end.
Cindy Sexton

Some say you didn't exist, some say you was too small to matter, and some even say it wasn't meant to be. I never got to see your face, I never got to hold you when you cried, and I never got to hear you call me mommy but, you are now my guardian angel and you are forever in my heart.
Cindy Sexton

Just like a butterfly, you received your beautiful wings.
Just like a butterfly, you flew away much to soon.
Just like a butterfly, you will always be precious.
Fly high my sweet butterfly and I will send you sweet butterfly kisses each day and night.
Cindy Sexton

Angel Kisses

I'm sending you kisses today but that's nothing new, I send you kisses everyday but your kisses are different because yours are angel kisses. Angel kisses are different than regular kisses because I send yours to heaven instead. I wish I could give you regular kisses but I can't so from now until I meet you in Heaven, I will send you angel kisses.
Cindy Sexton

A few verses I love:

Romans 9:11 - (For [the children] being not yet born, neither having done any good or evil, that

The purpose of God according to election might stand, not of works, but of him that calleth

Job 3:16 - Or as an hidden untimely birth I had not been; as infants [which] never saw light.

Isaiah 49:1 - The Lord called me from the womb, from the body of my mother he named my

name.

Deuteronomy 31:6

Be strong! Be courageous! Do not be afraid of them! For the Lord your God will be with you. He

will neither fail you nor forsake you.

The tattoo I got in memory of my Baby:

Since I was a little girl, I've always dreamed of having my own family. I use to play house and pretend I was pregnant.

I started trying to get pregnant at age 17 but never succeeded. In my early 20's, I started seeing a fertility Dr to see if something was wrong with me. They did a test to run Dye through my tubes to see if they were blocked. It turned out that both my tubes were blocked but they were able to unblock my right tube but said my left tube was infected and could become cancerous later if they don't remove it. The Dr said he would do all he could to try to repair my tube but said it was so bad that it was connected to my ovary and they had to completely remove my left tube and repair my ovary.

After my surgery, I spoke with my Dr to see about my chances of getting pregnant. The Dr told me that, I only had a 10% chance of ever conceiving a child and I would be considered high risk. He also advised me that it would be best to do invetro fertilization. I didn't have $12,000.00 to have that procedure done so in 2001, I walked away crushed thinking I would never be able to have a baby of my own.

I had to carry a needle with me for over 2 weeks and keep it in fridge or if I went somewhere had to keep it in cooler with ice. Went to Mississippi for a weekend trip 6 hrs away, went Friday night after work and had to drive back the next morning because I started my period so I had to be at the fertility clinic that day and give myself that shot so they could draw blood. Had many procedures done with the dye tests and many surgeries done to try to get tubes unblocked and my left one removed. After I finally got pregnant with the 1 tube and lost it, I gave up trying but, yes, I did all the ovulation tests and thermometer readings. The blood work was to test my egg cells, and that came back bad too. Not only am I dealing with 1 piece of a tube, my egg cells are bad too.

October 2005, I noticed some changes to my body and started feeling not right but I passed it off as being overworked from my job. Then Thanksgiving Day I was reaching for a pan out of the cabinet overhead and it fell out and hit my breasts, I started crying because it hurt so bad, they were very sensitive and sore but I didn't understand why. My oldest sister Cathy was there when this happened and she said, "Cindy I think you might be pregnant." I laughed at her thinking I wasn't but, I started thinking and realized that in October, I had my period but it was only for 1 day and only lasted about 2 hours and haven't had one since. I decided to go buy a pregnancy test the next day and I took it and to my surprise it was positive!! I called my sister and she said, your kidding with me, I said no its positive but I'm going to take another one to be sure. My sister then came over and after she got there, I did the 2nd test and it was positive. I was in shock and in disbelief, I was 27 years old and now I was finally going to have my dream come true.

December 1, 2005 I went for my 1st Dr visit to confirm pregnancy. The blood test came back that I was pregnant. I was considered high risk so; I had to go have ultrasounds and blood work done 2-3 times a week. Around December 6th I started spotting. I called the Dr and they put me on complete bed rest and said I need to be on bed rest for the rest of my pregnancy and they even was talking about hooking me up to monitors so they could keep an eye on me and the baby at all times. On December 11th I started cramping and hurting very bad in my lower stomach but I didn't think anything of it so I went to bed. I didn't really get any sleep that night because I kept tossing and turning all night. I got up to take my husband Mike to work and drank apple juice on the way but then had to stop to get sick. I was still hurting and cramping and just thought to myself "well, I guess this is the start of the morning sickness." After dropping my husband off at work, I went back home to lie down but I couldn't. At this point, I was hurting so bad that I couldn't sit, stand, or lie down because I was in so much pain. I couldn't eat anything all day and I also couldn't use the bathroom. I called the Dr and they said, "This is normal". My husband had to find a ride home after work because I couldn't stand to walk more less even sit in a car. After he got home from work, he noticed something wasn't right with me. I was on my hands and knees in bed with pillows stacked on pillows to rest my head on (this was the only way I could get comfortable) I was also swelled up and very pale. Mike fixed dinner and I think I took maybe 2 bites and couldn't eat anymore. I got up out of bed to try to go use the bathroom and ended up passing out in the hallway and could not get up because I was in so much pain. Mike called my sister and her husband to come help him with me. After they got there, they all told me they would pick me up and take me to the ER or an ambulance would come get me but either way, they said I was going to the ER!! They finally got me up and in the car and drove me to the ER. After getting there, the security guard looked at me and went to get me a wheel chair and took me straight back. I don't remember much from this point on other than what I was told but, they all said I was very pale and my eyes had already started rolling into the back of my head and the DR's told Mike that if he hadn't gotten me there when he did, I would have died. I ended up having a ruptured Ectopic pregnancy at 10 weeks gestation and had to have emergency surgery and had 18 staples in my stomach from surgery. I was in a room in the maternity ward for 3 days. Not 1 DR or nurse ever asked me how I was mentally and I was never given any information for grief counseling or anything. I left the hospital with empty arms and felt like I was all alone. On December 12, 2005, my life was forever changed.

Me and my husband Mike never knew the sex of our baby so we gave him/her the name of Baby Sexton.

I now run Facebook pages called:

"Ectopic Pregnancy Awareness"

https://www.facebook.com/ectopicpregnancyawareness

"Tender Moments Birthing Services"

https://m.facebook.com/TenderMomentsBirthingServices

"Our Shooting Stars Memorial Graphics"

https://m.facebook.com/profile.php?id=366183530173717

I am also taking online classes through stillbirthday.com to achieve my Doula certification (which I will be getting that this September 2014)

I will be offering services from Ft. Campbell Kentucky to Nashville Tennessee and all surrounding areas.

https://m.facebook.com/stillbirthday

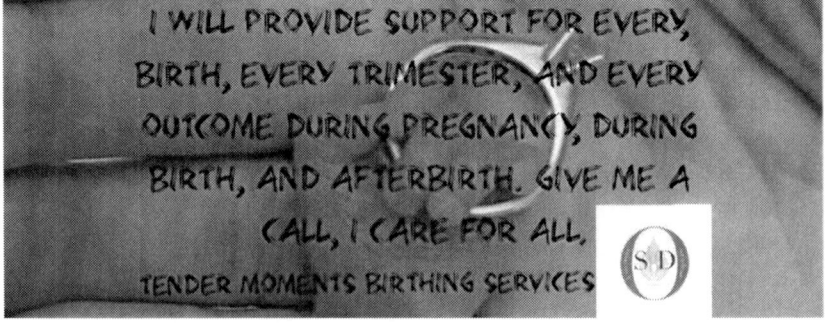

Cindy and Mike Sexton

I have 2 beautiful children, a boy and a girl, which to everyone else is enough, its a pigeon pair, you don't need any more.......but my dreams and my heart always wanted to have 5. We tried for number 3 for 18 months, much longer than the previous 2 had taken but we always let things go on knowing we would be blessed when the time was right.

5 days before Christmas 2013 I had a positive test. It was faint and took much longer to show than my previous pregnancies bit it was very early. I was so excited and decided to tell my husband on Christmas Day. On Christmas Eve I started bleeding, I just felt like something was wrong it was so hard to explain but I didn't sleep that night with worry. Christmas morning my daughter put on her 'big sister top' and we surprised my husband, an hour later I asked him to take me to the hospital.

The bleeding combined with aches and pains continued over Christmas and New Year, each day getting worse whilst the hospital would only allow blood tests every 48 hours to check rising hcg but no ultrasound. Following the New Year break I went and saw my gp for what should have been my first pregnancy related appointment, the booking of blood tests, ordering of future ultrasounds and refferal to an obstetrician. Instead she took one look at me and saw the anxiety in my eyes and ordered the ultrasound I had been begging the hospital for.

The ultrasound took place on a Thursday. The sonographer quite bluntly pointed out that there was nothing in my uterus, he could see nothing in my tubes and I was having a miscarriage. That was it, straight to the point, no emotion and don't forget to pay $90 on your way out......Messages were sent to family and friends that had been concerned to say there was no baby, we cried, we dealt, things happen and as long as everything was working there was hope to try again.

The next day started like all the previous over the past 2 weeks. Bleeding, pain, sucking it up and dealing because I was just having a painful miscarriage. That was until lunch time when my gp's office called and asked if I was still bleeding and if I had any pain. Of course I did! I had taken pain killers but was still hurting, I had 4 hours of work planned and working for myself there was no way I was going to cancel my day because of it. The gp went on to say that I needed to go to the hospital as soon as possible, my ultrasound showed fluid in my pelvic region, I was bleeding internally. The day before I had been told there was no baby now I was being told there was but it was in my tube which was starting to rupture....I was admitted to hospital on the Sunday after asking for a day to prepare my children for me to be admitted. I was admitted on the Sunday nil by mouth from midnight, I was told at 6pm that day that I would not be operated on until the following day so I could finally eat something. The following morning at 5am my tube completely ruptured, the pain was excruciating, morphine didn't help and I was rushed to surgery and had 2cms of my right tube removed and a drain placed for 24 hours to remove 2litres of blood from my pelvic area.

Life goes on, at least you are alive and you have 2 beautiful kids.....but it doesn't mean I didn't love the maybes and what ifs of the baby I had nick named Cricket. I could feel a piece of me was missing and I still so very badly wanted to be pregnant, to feel kicks and hiccups from inside and to have another child to love.

In March 2014 I found I was expecting again. The line showed the same on the test and I just knew.....I knew it wasn't right, my heart sunk as I prepared to tell my husband. This time we told no one, I went to my gp and explained that I just knew, she was understanding but still believed that the possibility of a second ectopic with 2 months was highly unlikely. I left with orders to go to the hospital over the weekend if I needed anything at all. The bleeding started on a Friday, on the Saturday morning I woke early and took myself off to the hospital, knowing there wasn't much that they could say or do. Despite being early on in this pregnancy they ordered an ultrasound based on my history. The ultrasound confirmed what I already knew in my heart, my baby (nick named Angel) was ectopic in my left tube. A whole new rotation of doctors were now working at the hospital. They gave me a choice of surgery to remove the entire left tube or Methotrexate injection. We chose surgery.....2 ectopic pregnancies within 2 months had left us raw, we needed to remove the possibility of any more heartache. The day we made our decision my husbands sister announced her 3rd pregnancy, she was currently 5 weeks pregnant with the exact same timing as me.

I am now left with 2 beautiful children, a boy and a girl, pigeon pair.....what more could any one want? Me I want a baby, I want to be pregnant, I want the what ifs and maybes, I want the morning sickness and indigestion, I want the kicks and hiccups, I want the first cuddle, first smile, first steps, first word, I want a full house and an even fuller heart. I want to feel normal again, I want to be the 28 year old that can fall pregnant naturally and not ever have to worry about things going wrong.

As the tears fall whilst finally getting a chance to tell my whole story, not needing to fake a smile as I say 'It's ok I have 2 great kids and there is always IVF in the future' I thank you with my whole heart Cindy for encouraging me to be brave and talk about ectopic pregnancy, not to hide in shame for the choices I have made or the feelings I have often felt the need to hide in front of others. I thank you for putting a spotlight on ectopic pregnancy and allowing me to connect with peers who have never shared their stories with me until now.

Angela Slattery

January of this year I missed my period. And I called the doctor and they told me to schedule an appointment like 6-8 weeks out end of Feb. Anyways I started spotting so I called them and they said oh everything is fine it's normal. Then the spotting turned into EXCESSIVE bleeding. Like nobody should bleed that much. I let myself bleed for a week and it just kept getting worse so one night me and my boyfriend were about to go to bed and I was going to go in the morning to the ER but his son woke us up coughing so we ended up going at like 2 am to the ER and I told them when they asked why I was here I said "possible miscarriage" I didn't know much if anything at all about Ectopic pregnancy. So they do some tests and what not and eventually tell me that I have a tubal pregnancy. And offered to have me do methotrexite instead of surgery. Doctor said surgery was too messy and he was sure this drug would work. Needless to say I got the drug. And I was due in for a check up the following Thursday. That day when I went to go get a check up. I was literally heading down the stairs when all of a sudden I was in the worst pain ever and my vision went white. I couldn't see anything and it was the middle of winter and I wasn't even cold. My boyfriend thought he would take a shortcut through the snow and he ended up getting stuck in the snow in the parking lot and tried t o get out of the snow for a good 20 minutes the whole time I was yelling at him to go back to the house and call 911 because it was bad. Eventually he called 911 and I couldn't even walk at that point because of the pain and they rushed me into the ER and spent like a good hour shoving needles in my arm couldn't find a vein for liquid because I was that dehydrated. I got surgery but this time it was by a different doctor. Not by the doctor who originally looked at me. Her name is Catharine roos at Hancock county obgyn in Greenfield Indiana and she saved my life. I got the surgery she just went in and did it no questions asked. And I appreciated that. I did not know the gender of the baby. Never heard the heartbeat. Just got 3 positive pregnancy tests. I recently signed up for wic too and only used one check before it all went down. I woke up from surgery (never been in surgery ever) in pain and really really thirsty. I had to learn to walk again because it was hard to walk because of the pain. She told me she removed the Left tube. And that I was internally bleeding. I could've died. Still makes me emotional talking about it and I still get those emails about how far along I would be today if that wouldn't have happened. I do not know if I will ever be able to have another child again. I have a son right now who is 5 years old. He might be my only baby. And that's really depressing to think about. It's been about 6 months since the surgery. I can start trying again not in pain. But I do have a scar that will never go away from it. Inside and outside. That's my story. Feel free to edit this so it's more legible. Thank you. Hope your book helps spread awareness around!

Elizabeth Long

I realized I was pregnant with my third child in December of 2012. I was ecstatic to be having another baby. It was around five weeks when I started having the pains. I didn't feel right; this wasn't something that happened in my other pregnancies. I was worried there was something wrong but I just shrugged it off and ignored my gut feeling. The pain only got worse from there, and then the bleeding started. I immediately went to see a doctor and told him from the start that I thought I was having an ectopic pregnancy but he didn't listen. No one listened, I didn't get the attention and support I needed, not from my husband, not from my doctor, not from anyone. I went through so many sleepless nights and anxiety attacks; I had never felt more alone in my entire life. My doctor told me I was having a miscarriage and I just needed to let it run its course. When I voiced my disagreement, he yelled and angrily told me that he could go in and remove one of my fallopian tubes for no reason. Then I got a call a few days later saying I had to go to the hospital for a methotrexate shot. So I went in and got the shot but, I still felt like something was terribly wrong. Two days after I had gotten the shot, I passed out with internal bleeding and I was rushed to the hospital. At the hospital I was being monitored for the rest of the day and night. The next morning I was rushed into surgery, I didn't know what to expect. When I awoke in the blank, depressing hospital room, I seeked out my husband and the look in his eyes told me what I needed to know. Not only had I lost my fallopian tube, cutting my chances of ever having a child again in half, but I had lost my precious little baby too. All of this could have been prevented if someone would have just listened to me in the beginning. I was seven weeks pregnant when I lost my baby and not a day goes by that I don't mourn my child. My little angel was taken from me before I could even hold her.

Unknown

To my child,

I am seven weeks pregnant with you, little one. I don't know you yet but, I already love you so much. I want more than anything to be able to hold you in my arms, come September 12. I do not know what tomorrow brings but, I do know that I am your Mommy and I will always love you with all my heart. I ache to hold you in my arms little one. Only God knows what's in store for us. It's all in Gods hands. If we can't meet now, I will see you in heaven one day soon, my sweet child. I am your Mommy and I will always be, know matter what. I love you with all my heart. I pray everyday that God will give us a chance together. It may not be our time together yet, I don't know. It's so hard to believe that everything in life happens for a reason. I will find out today, what our future holds together. I am so scared my child. I'm hurting so much inside. I would give anything in this world for you to be okay. I'm not sure why God would give you to me, and then take you from me. If you can tell God for me, to please give us a chance together. I promise to love you and always be a good Mommy to you. You hold my heart in your little hands, my sweet baby. I pray The Lord doesn't take you from me already. Whether we meet now or in heaven, please wait for your mommy baby. I love you so much always. Know that, you will forever be in my heart.

Love you always and forever

Your Mommy.

Jennifer Lopreato

Me and my husband had been trying to get pregnant for a month and I have been pregnant twice before so I knew my body and I knew I was I took a couple tests and it showed a faint line my husband said he couldn't see but I could I went to tons of pregnancy centers and they said the tests were negative but I spent hundreds of dollars' on home tests which showed a faint line I missed my period and felt pregnant. but then I started to spot on and off an felt weird I knew it was not a miscarriage but something was not right I called my obgyn they said go to er for an ultrasound they said they did not see anything so possible miscarriage but I knew I was pregnant three weeks later I took another home test there was a dark line no denying called me obgyn they did blood work said I was pregnant the next day I had pain and bleeding went to er they said possible miscarriage and sent me home next day I had pain and bleeding so bad I could not stand up I went to the er and they treated me like crap so why are you here what has changed in a day and were going to send me home luckily an ultrasound tech said there was to much "fluid" and they realized it was a burst ectopic and I was bleeding internally I was rushed into emergency surgery after they told me there was so much blood they couldn't see my abdomen at all It was a horrific amount of blood they said and the ectopic was still partially on my tube dangling down ripping it so they had to remove my left tube I woke up and they immediately sent me home. The whole situation was traumatic to me because I knew I was pregnant and I knew something was wrong for over 9 weeks but no one would listen to me not even my husband until it was too late. Now I am told I probably can't have any more kids but even If I can not to because with my previous health stuff it could kill me and other people don't understand its not just a miscarriage its not just surgery its both and now I can't try for the son me and my husband always wanted and no one understands my sadness. Not only that since the ectopic I have been in and out of the hospital with chronic abdominal pain and fatigue and now my thyroid is not working my heart has problems I have no stomach lining and a bunch of other issues and they think either the ectopic caused something or whatever caused the ectopic is in overdrive so in a year I have had major surgery lost a baby told I can't/shouldn't have any more kids and have been in pain and sick and no one understands. It is so sad other woman have had to go through similar things but it is nice that we can chat on the website and support each other because if you have not gone through this you can't even imagine. I would never wish this on anyone not even my worst enemy this has been a terrible experience it has made me stronger and appreciate life and my family more but I wish I could have done without this, and I hope my story can bring awareness that they need more support for woman going through this and they need to do more research to find out what causes ectopic and what not. Thanks for doing this book it is much needed.

Unknown

I have been married to my hubby for ten years... I never got pregnant on my own except one time and turn out to be a ectopic pregnancy I had the shot and the baby was gone that was in April 2008.. I never got pregnant again on my own... I had a friend who did IVF and had luck... So she told me to go to her doc and see if she can help me. So we went down there she did all kinds of test and everything looks great... We did our first transfer and it did not take I was devastating it did not take and then the second one it took... They implanted two eggs Everything looks good and when I went to the doc for the us and they could not find a heartbeat and again I miscarriage I was 5 1/2 weeks I took the pills and I was in labor until 8 Fri night when I finally pass the baby in the toilet.. I was devastating.... So I wait to try again so I went down and try again this they implanted three eggs again I was pregnant... No problem with the pregnancy expect pain on the right side.... That sun I went to see my dad and I was hurting real bad... I came home and I was bleeding and hurting real bad... I went to bed and woke up with severe pain... I went to the er and they did a us and find out my tube on my right side burst and I was bleeding to death.... I had two eggs was in my uterus... I had a emergency surgery to get me to stop bleeding and take out both of my tubes... I still was pregnant with the two... I got out the hospital on a wed and thurs night I was miscarriage the other two again back to the er and the hospital on that Fri I had a D&C... I was devastating.... I about lost my life and now my lovely sister us going to carried a baby for me since I can't do it because it will kill me.....

Unknown

On the 23rd of May I went to a & e with really bad cramping and bleeding id had it for 2 weeks on and off but had no explanation why I had blood test urine samples and the nurse told me I was pregnant and the pain and bleeding was just because I had a water infection I was over joyed because it was all i ever wanted I couldn't wait to ring my friends and boyfriend.

 A week had past and the pain seemed to be getting worst and the pain was really bad on the left side so days I could barley walk on the 3rd of June I rang nhs direct and was sent to a walk in centre where the doctor told me I could be miscarrying or it could be an eptopic pregnancy I was sent to the early pregnancy unit at half 3 in the morning I was by myself scared and alone. The nurse came in and gave me an internal examination but she couldn't see what she was looking for so booked me in for a scan in the morning.

8.30am came and I was sent for my scan the nurse scanned my belly but couldn't see the baby and thought maybe that was because the baby was only 5 weeks 1 day so she decided to give me a internal scan and she was pushing hard on the left side of me and I knew then it wasn't good news the pain was horrific, tears rolled down my face.

She told me to go into the waiting area where a doctor came up to me and sat down and told me it was an ectopic pregnancy and The baby was in the left tube and I needed to be admitted for an operation to remove my baby and left tube my whole world fell apart I asked the doctor if she could move the baby and put it where it was suppose to be an she said it was impossible I was so desperate and wanted my baby more than anything.

A few hours past and I was sent to the operating theater tears still streaming down my face all alone I was put to sleep and the operation begun. I remember waking up in terrible pain feeling sick with the nurses round me asking me if I was ok but I just felt numb. I was taken back on to the ward where my friend was there waiting for me as he sat down I told him my baby's gone as he comforted me I knew nothing could hurt like this then my boyfriend came and the doctor came too, everything was moving too fast and he told me that he was surprised I wasn't in worst pain the baby was quiet big in my tube and that it had ruptured and the baby was removed and my left tube too. it all happened to quick I just wanted to go home but I had to eat walk and use the toilet before they let me go home I struggled up out of bed in agony making myself walk forcing the food down me so I could just home I didn't want to be there anymore an hour later I was home I couldn't stop crying I crawled into bed holding my tummy wishing things were different at that moment I realized nothing could ever hurt like this. The next morning I didn't feel pregnant my breast weren't sore anymore And that horrible pain I had wasn't there anymore but I would of given anything to just have it back and my baby people said you can get pregnant again and have another but I wanted that pregnancy and my baby.

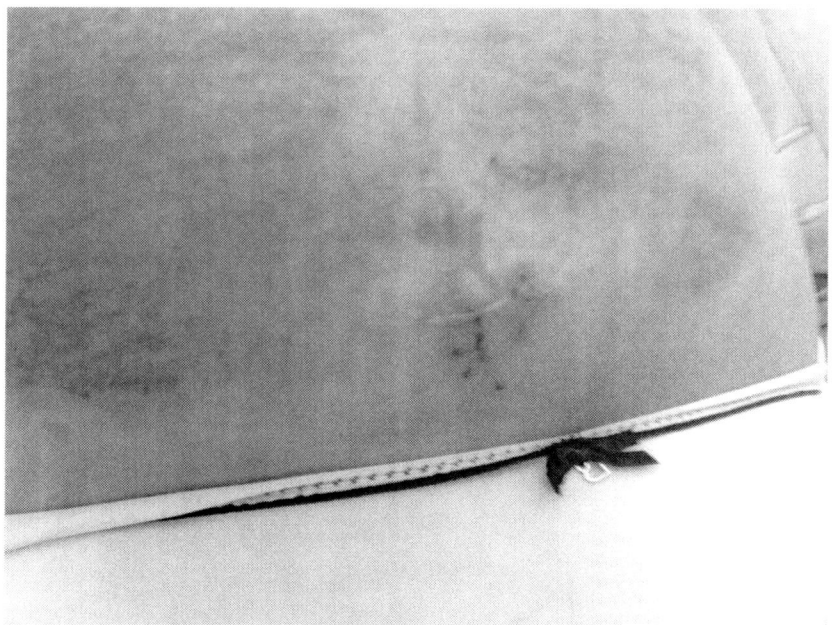

Maxine Bindi

February 15th 2011 I was at work where I worked as a receptionist in a Hotel. I was near the end of my shift when I doubled over in pain. I later went to hospital where I was examined and later sent home having been told to go home and rest and come back the following day to have a scan. I was just over 7 weeks pregnant but had no blessing so I was convinced it would be ok. I already had a 5 year old little boy with a normal pregnancy. When I returned the next day for a scan with my husband I was so sure it was just routine to check as by now the pains were not as bad. I was told that my baby was ectopic and I would need an emergency op in the next hour. I was devastated and in total shock. I signed the consent forms after being told of the risks. I cried all the way to theatre where they removed my Right tube after it ruptured during the operation. After suffering a miscarriage 8 months later I finally fell pregnant again and I have a beautiful 17 month old baby girl and my beautiful 7 year old son Not a day goes by when I don't think about the baby that I lost.

Debbie

I was 9 weeks pregnant and I started to have pain on my right hand side and a brown discharge, it was a Saturday so I got an appointment with an emergency Dr.....she didn't take my blood pressure or anything she just went into a story about how common miscarriages are and I should wait 48 hours to see if I miscarry. I made the 48 hours after bed rest and was delighted.....the next day I suffered what I can only explain as the most severe pain I have ever felt and was crippled with pain....I passed out through the pain and fell against the toilet knocking myself out. I got rushed to hospital where the pain decreased......I had an internal scan (whilst constantly vomiting) my mum actually asked the question 'is she having an ectopic pregnancy?' Only to be told no I wasn't as the sac had developed, I was then put in a hospital bed to stay over night. My mum and husband stayed until 9pm so I could get some rest, when mum was leaving I asked her to just tell the nurse I had a pain in my right shoulder (internal bleeding) my mum actually asked if she should stay to be told that it wasn't necessary I was fine. Once they left the pain increased quickly and I became doubled in pain.....a nurse did my blood pressure which had dramatically dropped, within minutes I was being prepped for surgery....the pain became so intense that I screamed every time they pushed the bed over a small bump. I was taken to surgery and operated on for 6 hours as it ruptured severely and I lost huge amounts of blood.....so much so that I had to have a blood transfusion the following day. The pregnancy had reached the end of the tube and got stuck and therefore I had a partial tube removal. The second time I had a scan at 6 weeks which couldn't find if it was in the right place, I then had blood tests for the next 4 weeks followed by another scan. The Dr said 'I have found a heartbeat.......but it is in the wrong place'. I was then prepped for key hole surgery, unfortunately while I was under anesthesia the tube ruptured and they could not reach it due to the scar tissue from the first ectopic.....they called the consultant into the surgery and he found that my Bowel was fused to my stomach from the scar tissue and he eventually took everything out in order to get to the burst tube. Obviously now I am unable to have children and they have recommended that I do not attempt ivf due to the risk of not being able to reach the baby

Nicola Akers

As this is a still sore topic I have only just felt the courage to tell my story.

Over a year ago I met the boy of my dreams, blue eyed, blonde hair and a smile to kill. A love struck girl who had come out of a string of bad relationships. In the first couple of months we fell deeply in love. We used to joke about kids how they would have his blue eyes or my freckles while hand in hand strolling through the park. At 26 and still both living at home we planned we would start a family straight away when we had the money. But fate had already decided before me.

About 6 months into dating I went on holiday with my brother and family. I felt strange the entire week tired, sick not quite there. I could feel my body was changing so while we were away I nipped to the pharmacy to get a pregnancy test. Sure enough two feint lines appeared. I rang up my boyfriend shaking; we were both overjoyed about the result. After my holiday I went back home and we hugged and rejoiced. I went to the doctors he was pleased and said to us "now all you have to do is wait for your scan" sending me off with paper. That's odd, I thought. Surely they need to check me more but he just asked me to get a digital test and tell him how far along I was. I was eight weeks. All this time I hadn't realized.

Two weeks later at ten weeks my boyfriend and I were strolling through town looking at baby clothes dreaming of our children. I started to get stabbing mild pains in my right side. I hunched. I said I need to go home and rest so we went back. Before long I was crying with pain. My partner rang the ambulance and they came. I was screaming loudly on the floor at this point so unconscious I had no idea where I was till I was on oxygen in an ambulance. The a & e was dark and dingy. I felt terrified. They drugged me up with morphine and left me in a corner. I held my boyfriends hand and sobbed. I knew something was wrong with our baby. So did he. Furious he kept shouting for staff but nobody came. Eventually drugged on morphine and codeine and exhausted with pain I dosed off. I awoke to find a doctor there. My boyfriend looked furious. The doctor did A few blood tests and the told me I was fine. Are you pregnant? He asked yes I said crying. Ill book you for a scan next Tuesday. He told me to leave because I was taking up bed space. Angry and upset I went home. I slept all day popping painkillers like they were smarties but again the next evening the pain reared its head. I went to another a & e was told nothing was wrong and told to go home. Before Tuesday came I was taken to the different hospital again I was bleeding heavily like a period but much worse, with pains my right leg, my leg had gone limp, my color was pale as a ghost and I'd been loosing weight like crazy. I was so weak I had to be wheeled into hospital and into the scan room. I knew I had miscarried in my head. "There's no baby in the womb" she said news I solemnly knew already, my blonde angel was dead. "It's in your tube" she said "what?" I said gasping. She ran out the room looking startled. Shortly after I was rushed into a stretcher bed. "If we don't operate on removing your tube now you won't live past tomorrow" said the surgeons. You would have thought I would be afraid but I wasn't. As they prepped me up for surgery I prayed to die. I didn't want to live without my baby.

Weeks and months afterwards I still longed to die, I self harmed and overdosed on painkillers. Death seemed the only thing to stop the pain. If it wasn't misery it was alcohol addiction. Very off character for me. Eventually I saw that my misery was making my boyfriend suffer too. Although he never spoke about his sadness all I had done for months was cry to him and tell him I wanted to die, tell him I hated myself and I was a ruined woman, a waste of a female with no tube, practically a man, ugly and worse names I called myself, I gave myself a verbal beating everyday, It was killing him to the point he was off work with depression. I had to stop. I had to be strong for him. This is the Boy I fell in love with, the boy who loved every dimple and freckle on my face every smile I used to give him. The boy who loved me more than the universe. I got a new job and began therapy sessions to deal with my manic depression. I didn't take my pills but the CBT was really helping the one to ones where I could just cry and cry and talk to a random lady but she was my release every Wednesday.

Now another 8 months on my partner and I are back to the loved up couple we used to be. The situation has made us stronger. We both have new jobs and are saving for a house and a puppy, we both adore huskies. I am on the implant to give my body and soul healing time from this ordeal but most importantly I have changed doctors and hospitals. My new doctor is fabulous and monitors me regularly. I also will be considered a high risk pregnancy next time which means monitoring every step and an early scan. Having good doctors would have meant this never would have happened. But I'm not angry. I'm just more clued up. Thank you for listening to my story.

Marnie

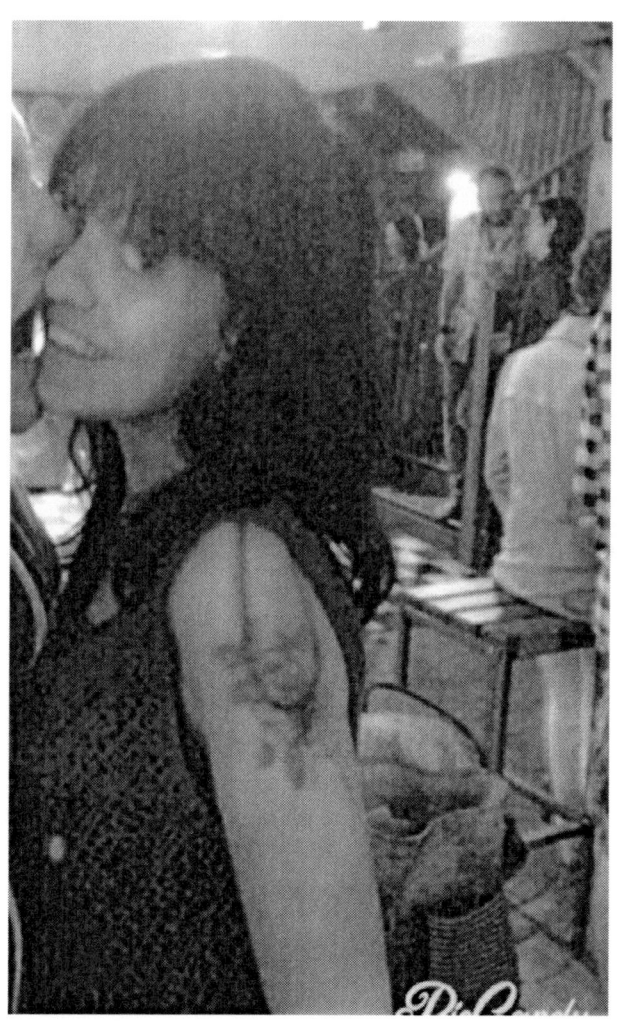

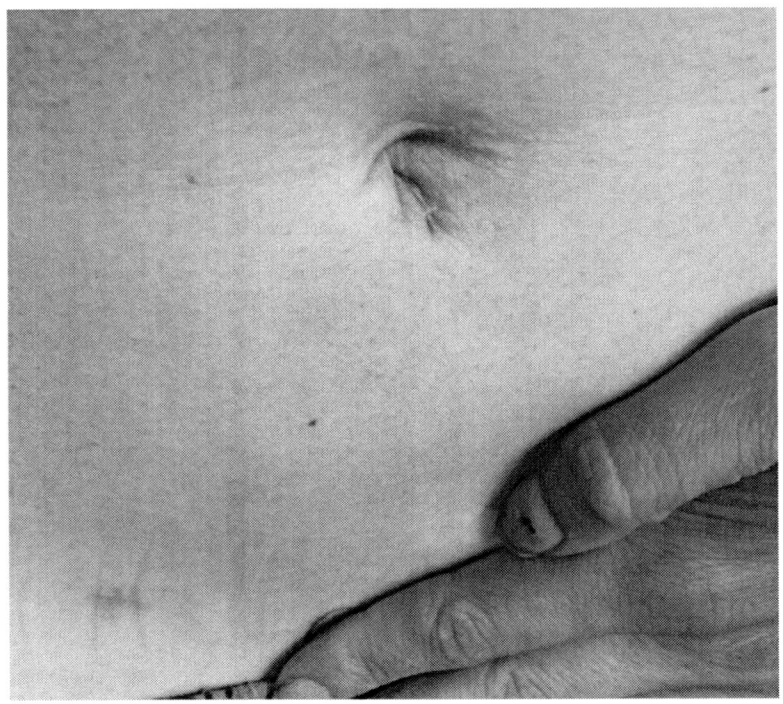

Marnie

My name is Roisin McGlinchey (nee Hunter) I live in Strabane, Co. Tyrone. I am aged 32. I am happily married to my husband Johnny for over two years now, but been together 14 years in total so we have shared these emotional losses together, and other eventful experiences. We have no children. The support and advise I have received from my family has been overwhelming. I have two lovely sisters I am the eldest, then Sinead then Claire, without their help I would never have come through the experiences I faced.

I have had three ectopic pregnancies. Here is my story. My first ectopic was six months after the sudden lost of my father in May 2010 (7th). In the early hours of the morning I presented myself at the A&E Department, Altnagelvin Hospital, Derry I had right sided lower abdominal pain, I knew I was at the early stages of pregnancy and was afraid. When I had an ultrasound scan it was confirmed it was an ectopic pregnancy and I was rushed to theatre for emergency surgery, my right tube was removed as it ruptured. This was an emotional roller-coaster and it took me several months to recover.

After several checkup appointments and meetings with my consultant It was decided it was safe enough for me to try again as everything appeared normal and my fertility was good.

In between getting my head around my first ectopic I sadly lost my mother suddenly as well on the 10th April 2011. So now I was grieving for my dad, my baby first baby and my dear mother.

On the 13th October 2012 I attended at my local A&E again but this time I had three urinary pregnancy with all the same result 'Negative'. I did not know I was pregnant. The fear in my head was saying I am not pregnant I cant be its negative, thank god it not another ectopic pregnancy. However the nightmare come soon after this when it was confirmed it was another ectopic pregnancy in my left side this time and I required surgery again. This time it was an un-ruptured tubal pregnancy and my left tube was saved.

Sadly on the 27th February 2014 I was taken into hospital again I was complaining of a right side abdominal pain I had no bleeding or other symptoms. I did not even know I was expecting another baby, a few hours later It was confirmed it was another ectopic pregnancy in my left tube, I was taken in for surgery this was emergency surgery cause at this stage I had internal bleeding , however when they where carrying out the procedure the left tube showed no evidence of an ectopic, instead my 3rd ectopic was in the stump part of my right Fallopian tube, this I was told was extremely unusual. This stump and my baby was removed.

Currently I am waiting on an appointment to meet with my Consultant to discuss what the future holds for me and family. I am still in the grieving process and sometimes I think more positively than others, but I do not think my life will be complete until I have a little baby McGlinchey.

Regards and thanks for the opportunity to share my story.

Thanks in advance. Roisie McGlinchey

Roisie McGlinchey

Hi my name is Jane Smith, and I would like to share my ectopic story.

Although it has been thirteen years ago, it still seems as if it were yesterday. My story doesn't seem as traumatic as other ones that I have read, however it was a very scary time for my family and I. It was June 2001, and my husband Spencer and I found out that we were expecting our second child. We already had a healthy two year old little boy, Nelson, who was the apple of our eye. I had already suffered a miscarriage nine months before, when my son was just 15 months old. Although devastating, it was anything compared to the miscarriage that was yet to come.

In June of 2001, I was expecting again, baby number 2. From the beginning, I just didn't feel good. Looking back now, I knew something just wasn't right. I was very sick at my stomach and had aches and pains that I just couldn't explain. I went to the doctor, but only for a pregnancy confirmation. Since I had had no real complications before, there wasn't really any need to do an early ultrasound or investigations. A few weeks went by. I still didn't feel well but blamed it on normal pregnancy woes. I did have severe lower back pain, which afterwards I did find out was an ectopic symptom. At about the 9 week mark, I woke up in the middle of a Thursday night. I firmly believe that The Lord woke me up and from there began to prepare me for what was to follow the next week.

Upon waking I went to the bathroom to discover light pink spotting. Upset I woke my husband who comforted me and told me that it would be ok. The weekend came and The spotting got heavier and turned into a period. My doctor told me to rest and put my feet up. Sunday morning rolled around and the bleeding was heavier. I ended up going to Decatur General ER, where the doctor met me. Upon examination he just assumed miscarriage and advised me to go home and rest and call the office in the morning for an ultrasound. Let me stop here and say that there wasn't an ultrasound tech at the hospital that morning. Had there been one, it would have made things much quicker and easier. I went home and rested. Monday morning which was now into July 2001, I woke up very sick. My son and I were home alone as my husband had gone to work. To speed it up here, I became very sick, with nausea, and passing blood clots the size of leeches. I called my mother immediately to come and take me to the doctor. Upon her arrival to my house, I was lying in the bathroom floor feeling like I was hanging on to life by a thread. My blood pressure was dropping rapidly and causing my fainting spells. My mother and my two year old little boy took me to the doctor's office that was full of pregnant women that day. I was a hot mess. When called back, I got up and fainted in the floor. They ordered an ultrasound which only revealed blood clots breaking loose and passing. The tech for whatever reason never looked at my Fallopian tubes.. Because I was so very sick, my doctor afraid that I was dehydrated sent me to the hospital. Again while in triage I fainted. My blood pressure bottomed out so low they tilted my head back to elevate my feet, which later proved to be an almost fatal mistake. My doctor came and did an exam. A dnc was performed that afternoon and if I was feeling better I could go home afterwards. After the dnc the nurse sat me up to go to the bathroom and I again fainted. She and my mother both insisted that I didn't need to go home. I was admitted and stayed that night. The next morning, my hematocrit levels were checked and found to be very low. I was still bleeding and my doctor puzzled. I also was very labored in my breathing and felt like a knife was sticking under my ribs. An ultrasound was ordered and this time my doctor and the tech were present to see what was going on. The look on my doctors face said oh my goodness. The ultrasound revealed a 10cm mass where my right Fallopian tube was supposed to be and it had ruptured. I had no abdominal pain. Just a few bouts of fainting and heavy bleeding. Within 20 minutes I again was in surgery. I was cut open to remove the ruptured ectopic pregnancy and my right Fallopian tube. I also required 4 pints of blood.

The next morning which was July 4, 2001, the nurse noticed a cough that I had and my breathing was labored. X-rays revealed that the bottom lobe of my lungs were saturated with blood, hence the almost fatal mistake of lowering my head and raising my feet in the er. My O2 stats level was low 80s. Not good. Into the icu I went for 2 days. Lots of oxygen masks and pokes and prods it was. It was a scary time for me and my husband, but The Lord took care of it all. By Saturday I was on the mend enough to go home. I was weak but thankful.

For the next 5 years after that, Spencer and I became content with one child. I knew my chances of having another child were less than what they used to be. In February of 2004, we would find out that we were expecting baby number 2. I was nervous and my doctor was too. My daughter was in the right place growing and we welcomed her in October of that year. When she was 10 months old, we found out that we were expecting baby number 3. In May of 2006 we welcomed our second son. Today they are 15, 9 and 8. I will never forget that week, thirteen years ago. It is encouraging to me to be able to offer hope and encouragement to others who are facing or have faced an ectopic pregnancy.. Thanks for letting me share my story and God bless

Jane and Spencer Smith
Ardmore, TN

Our story starts when I met my current husband in 2011; we had known each other for many years before we had got together.

I already had 2 children from a previous marriage aged 8 and 12 but Thinking that this marriage would last a life time and feeling fulfilled with the 2 children I had, I was sterilized shortly after my 8 year old was born.

Myself and my new partner talked about having children as he had no children of his own, I explained my fertility situation but really thought there was nothing that could be done to change the fact that I could no longer have children naturally. Until we began to look at what options their where available out there.

We planned and booked into a private hospital to talk about and go ahead with a tubal reversal, as this would give us opportunity to become pregnant naturally.

So in September 2012 I had my surgery but they could only repair one tube the other they had to remove, and after just 2 weeks we where able to begin to try for a child we so dearly wanted, we where so excited, then on 14th January 2013 I was so excited and could wait to test as my monthly cycle was late, I rushed out to buy a test "woohoo" it was positive, though the line was very faint which I assumed it was just because I tested early. We decided to nickname our baby "baby pip"

10 days later I awoke to a sharp pain on one side shooting down my leg and a pain from my shoulder down my arm, something did not feel right. We attended to my local A&E first thing in the morning and explained of the pain I had and they I had recently been through a tubal reversal, they took some bloods and booked me in at the early pregnancy unit later that day to be checked out and more bloods. They checked me out with a early scan but said they could not see a baby so was unsure what was wrong until the results came back from my blood tests, so they would ring me up later that evening, it felt like forever waiting for them to ring back, constantly checking my phone and waiting.

That evening the phone rang, I answered the phone feeling anxious about what to expect, they explained that the results defiantly suggested that I was pregnant but due to not seeing a baby on the scan they thought that possibly it was ectopic, so wanted to go into hospital straight away that evening and stay in so that they could keep a close eye on me and take more bloods first thing in the morning to compare.

I packed my over night case and off to the hospital I went.

The next morning 25th January 2013 I had some more bloods taken which where rushed through to receive results ASAP. When the results came back they confirmed that the pregnancy was still on going and growing well as my levels have more than doubled over the night. But I needed to have another scan to look where the pregnancy was growing.

They sent me to the scanning unit, (I felt sick with worry hoping that all would be ok) we looked at the screen and could see our little baby and the heart beating away and was dated at 10 weeks pregnant,

(Our baby pip)For them couple of seconds I was so happy like any new mum to be would be, the. Just for that happiness to snatch away from us, (They explain that our little baby was a ectopic pregnancy, and I would have to have surgery straight away to remove and end the pregnancy meaning also to remove my remained tube) we didn't have time even for this to sink in, before I was taken off ready for surgery.

When I came Around, they spoke about it to us like it was just every day surgery to them, they never talked to us like we had just lost a baby, (was this just because I was only 10 wks I asked myself? Surely A baby is a baby regardless of how many weeks pregnant you are, but why do they not see it like that?) they just told us everything was fine and all went well, like we where expected not be affected, the surgery was done so we could just be sent home later that day to get in with things as normal, we weren't even offered counseling.

We returned home and over the next few days it hit me hard, I felt all I did was cry, I couldn't focus on anything, all I wanted was our baby back, I felt like it was my fault, it was my body that that caused the pregnancy to be ectopic, I felt a failure as a women, and why would my partner want to be with me anymore when I could no longer give him a child he longed for.

I found it hard to face people after but what I think hurt most was the fact that a lot of people would never discuss what happened; it was like our baby had just been forgotten about. But I now understand that it was hard for them to, to find the right words, as sometime words don't seem enough to express how sorry you are for what's happened.

As time went by it became easier to deal with our loss, we made a memory box with our baby pips scan picture and placed in a little teddy with angle wings, which I keep with my other children's memory boxes, we also have a framed scan picture in the house, which I can now look at and smile, without the tears.

I attend the church where my brother is buried and always place on flowers for my brother and my little baby pip as I know he will be keeping him safe, waiting for that one day where we shall meet. The memories are always there, and not a day goes by that I don't think about our baby pip, but the pain does get easier.

I can only speak for myself on how it was personally for me after, but I do know my partner was also distraught about the situation, but he was also my rock throughout and we held each other together at times of need, we shared our thoughts and feelings and helped each other through no matter how painful, it brought us closer together and made us stronger as a couple.

Now on 16th July 2014 we have some fantastic news to share, thought it's been a emotional roller coaster along the way, but very much worth it, we are currently 14 wks pregnant through ivf, and are happy to say that all is going well.I would like to thank my loving husband for all his support throughout, he is my rock I truly don't know what I would of done without him, not only is he my husband, but my best friend and my soul mate. Words cannot describe how much he means to me.

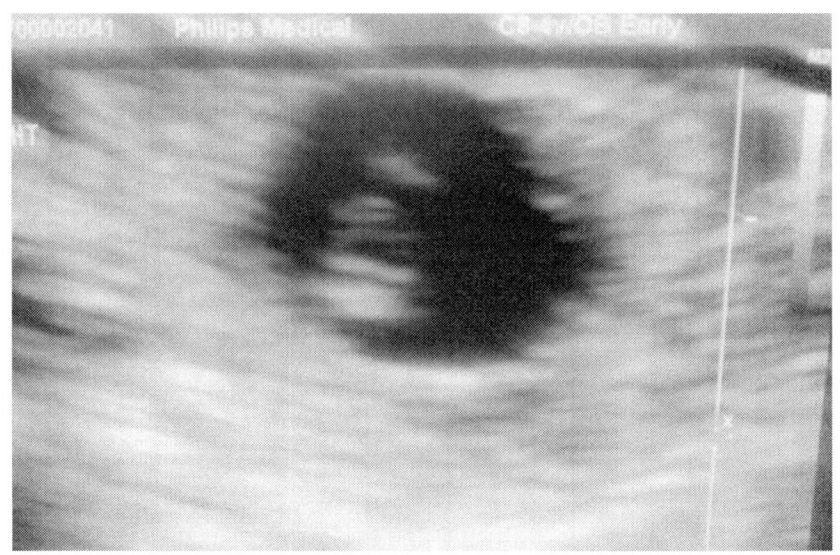

Louise & Micheal Kitts

Me and the hubby met in March 2009 and we moved In together April 2009, we got engaged 2nd July 2009 and was ready to spend the rest of our lives together. We we're madly in love. We started to plan our lives out together and things we're just perfect. We bought a puppy for our home and the only thing that was missing was a wedding ring and a baby. Around September time we decided we would start trying to conceive, so October came, the. November, then December and before we knew it was February 2010 and we had no baby still. We decided to go and see a doctor and he referred us to a fertility specialist for help. We arrived at the appointment and answered what seemed like a thousand questions but he smiled all the way through which have is hope. He referred me to have dye put through my tubes to check they we're clear and tested my husband's sperm. All came back clear and good. At our next appointment he was going to put me on Clomid. In March 2010 on a Sunday night I had an awful pain in my right side of my head and my husband took me to a&e and I was diagnosed with a blood clot on the brain. They operated and removed the clot and diagnosed me with idiopathic inter cranial hypertension. I rescheduled my fertility appointment and was under a neurological consultant at the hospital. At my appointment with the fertility clinic he told us as I had an ongoing condition he could not help until I had the all clear, this broke our hearts as it's a condition for life. We decided to plan our wedding. In May 2010 I had another blood clot and we decided to move the wedding to September 2010. We were happy that we had each other but we had a piece missing. We went on to have a devastating miscarriage in June 2011 at 11 weeks. We decided to concentrate on each other in February 2012 I had an awful pain in my right side and right shoulder tip. I phoned nhs direct and the nurse did a phone assessment and assured me I was fine. All this time we hadn't even realized I had missed a period. The next morning I went to my local doctor as I wasn't happy with the phone consultation and they did a urine test and referred me straight to the hospital as possible ectopic. I had a internal scan and ectopic was confirmed. We was devastated again. I collapsed 30 minutes later on the ward and was rushed straight to theatre as my right tube had ruptured. I ended up having my right tube removed and lost my life twice that afternoon. When I can round I was told by the doctor I was 8 weeks and 4 days into my pregnancy. I wasn't allowed to work for 6 weeks while I healed. As time went on me and my husband shut down and stopped communicating and we ended up separating. I am now just starting to rebuild my life but my heart will always yearn for he baby that never became. I lost my tube, my heart, my life, my baby and my marriage.

Anonymous

My name is Tiffany . I am married. I have two children, both of which prior to marriage.\My fiancé

and I found out we were expecting August 23, 2013. My due date was 4-21-14. Which was

my mother's birthday.   She had died when I was 6 due to a car wreck. Three weeks later I was

rushed to the emergency room to find out our pregnancy was eptopic and the doctors would have

to do immediate surgery to remove my left fallopian tube. The news was unbearably

heartbreaking. My husband had experienced this before through a previous relationship in which

his partner left him. The depression I went through after our loss was at an all time high, we pray

to have a baby in the future, but the loss of our little one will always be in our hearts, however

long it takes to truly heal.

Tiffany

I was 19 years old and been married for 4 months. My husband had took a job in Texas so I mostly stayed in a hotel while he worked. I went through a period where food made me sick every time I ate I would vomit my breast were tender and I missed my period I had taken several test that all came back negative. So I figured I was just having female issues since I had a past of endometriosis. One morning I woke up in extreme pain and bleeding through a pad every 25-30 mins. I was crying and in indescribable pain. My husband took me to the ER. They did a pregnancy test. The nurse came in told me I was pregnant and in the same sentence said now we got to find out why your losing it, I was devastated. I had things done to be that I later found out shouldn't have been done on a pregnant woman they told me that I was trying to miscarry and put me on bed rest. They gave me pain Meds and phenegan and sent me on my way. The next morning I woke up literally in my own blood. I had bled so badly it had gone through the pad, sheets and soaked in the mattress I could hardly walk. I was taken by ambulance to another hospital where I was told I had miscarried and was pregnant again, they sent me on my way and put me on bed rest. I ended up going in and out of consciousness. My husband was so afraid I was going to die he quit his job and literally flew us back home to Ringgold, Georgia the next day. There several tests were run and they came to the conclusion that I was pregnant and it was most likely dead. I was scheduled for emergency surgery Nov 21,2007 the day after my birthday. I woke up from surgery and was told I had an ectopic and they removed it. My baby was 3 inches long and as big around as a cherry tomato I lost my right Fallopian tube later down the rd from this pregnancy. My Dr told me if my husband had not gotten me home I would have died with in a week. I went through a lot. I had lost a baby 6 months prior to my ectopic To a miscarriage so this was hard, and I was made to feel that a ectopic was not a real pregnancy. Me and my husband will be hopefully trying for a baby in the next 6 months. I feel I went through this for a reason and I hope my story helps someone!

Thanks for your time

Katie Carroll

My husband and I were so excited when I did a home pregnancy test and the result was positive, having being diagnosed with PCOS (poly cystic ovarian syndrome) we were told that falling pregnant would be harder to do. We decided to wait a while before going to the doctor just in case it was a false reading and a week later on the 21 April 2014I took another home pregnancy test which was also positive. We went to the doctor the next day where he performed an ultra sound and told me yes the test shows I'm pregnant but he cannot see anything in my womb so it must still be too early to detect.

On the 28th of April I started experiencing severe pain I could not walk or get out of bed after a few hours I started to bleed I phoned my husband who took me back to the doctor. He said some bleeding is normal and the pain sometimes happens when the baby is settling into the womb and he asked me to come in a week later. That same evening the pain got worse and I knew something was definitely wrong so my husband took me to the emergency room. Once there they decided to admit me because they were not sure what was going on and had to wait for me to be looked at by a gynecologist. So I laid in that bed and waited and waited but the doctor did not come that night or the next morning I began to vomit and my pain got worse and worse and still no doctor my husband decided to go and complain to the sisters on duty who were less than helpful. Eventually the doctor arrives at 13:00pm and performs a vaginal scan when he sees nothing he books me in for surgery. I was in shock I didn't know what was going on I didn't realize they would be ripping my baby out of me

My surgery took place at 18:00pm that night a laparoscopy with salpingostomy where they slut the tube and remove the baby I came out if surgery at 21:30pm that night with severe low bp when I woke up the next morning and was told that my baby was in my tube and I was about 4 weeks pregnant I broke down. How could this happen? How could God take my baby? Why me? It was very difficult for me to accept. It still is. After 5 days in the hospital I was sent home to recover. Recover physically from the stitches and pain but how was I to recover emotionally? This was the hardest thing in the world for my husband and I to go through I felt so alone and even guilty that my body betrayed me and killed my baby I did not even want to look in the mirror. After about 6 weeks I started dealing with what happened emotionally with the support of my family who I would not have survived without. And finally was on the road to recovery. Then on the 23 May 2014 I started feeling ill that horrible pain was back and this time it was so much worse I started passing huge blood cloths about the size of my hand I knew something was terribly wrong. My husband phoned my doctor who performed the operation he said it's probably my first period after the operation. The pain got worse and I was almost passing out when my husband decided to rush me back to the hospital. Once there another urine test is done and they tell me I'm pregnant. I tell them I just had my baby ripped out of me due to ectopic pregnancy and my husband and I have not been intimate since they acted like I was lying. Then a blood test (my first blood test) this showed my hgc levels to be around 30000 I was admitted again

The doctor who performed the operation comes to see me the next day and tells me what possibly happened was when the operation was done some tissue could have been left behind and it grew . That's it no apology nothing he prescribed me to take 20 methotexrate the next day . I felt like dying how could this happen again. How could I loose my baby twice and be expected to live why he didn't check my hgc levels after the operation how could he do this to me and still be so cold to me. I took the tablets and stayed in hospital for a further 6 days. After I was discharged I had to go for weekly blood tests to monitor my levels

No one understood the pain I felt or the sense if loss it was a pain I felt worse than death but thanks to Gods grace I'm still standing and will continue to do so every day . Even though some days are better than others and sometimes when the pain is too much to bare and I feel like ending it all I think of my little one in heaven and want him/ her to be proud of me .i want to be the kind of person they would have been proud to call mum .

Written by Adell Melissa Naicker
Ectopic Pregnancy Survivor

I've experienced five tubal pregnancies. No tubes remaining. No live births for me, but the maternal love remains. God has other plans for me. I will see my babies one day. Their souls are safe in heaven waiting on me.

Anonymous

Hi My name is Melissa Charbonneau I live in Tampa, Florida and I am 37 years old. My husband Chris is 38 and we have been married 9 years and together 16. He is my everything and my rock, I don't know what I would do without his support. I had my first ectopic pregnancy in January 2013. We first thought that it was a miscarriage, but the Dr. now believes that it was an ectopic that miscarried on its own. I was of course devastated, but thought well at least I know that my husband and I can get pregnant. A couple weeks later my best friend called to tell me she was pregnant with her second child. I of course was happy for her, but it still is just hard to hear and I know it was hard for her to tell me too. My second ectopic was in August 2013. I had a dnc done to see if there was any tissue in the uterus and there was not, so I was given a shot of methotrexate. I had no idea what this was until after it was already administered to me. I was very surprised to find out that it is a chemotherapy drug. In the following days, weeks, months it was very apparent to me. My hair started to fall out more than usual, my skin wasn't normal, and I got sick with everything that was going around. My immune system was shot and I ended up with pneumonia. This time I took it even worse and went into a complete depression and had to seek help from a physician. I was put on Lexapro and after some time the crying and utter sorrow got less and less. The next month I had to plan and throw my best friends baby shower. I was excited to see her and give her our special present. My husband and I made her a beautiful rocking horse for her new little girl. We worked on it for almost a month, it is beautiful. During that time I was dealing with my depression and would cry after working on the gift just about every day. It was knowing that we could be making this for our child that would have been born around the same time that was killing me inside. I did make it through the shower without having an emotional melt down, thankfully. It took me 6 months to be emotionally ready to try again and I was scared to death that it was going to happen again. I found out the last week of March that I was pregnant again. I was very excited, but afraid. My Dr. monitored me right away at 5 weeks, taking blood work every other day. The blood work looked great and was doubling just like it is supposed to. A week and a half later my husband and I went to our appointment for my transvaginal ultrasound. The ultrasound technician was looking and looking and my eyes just started welling up with tears, I just knew that the baby was not in my uterus again. As the tears rolled down my face, my husband held my hand tightly and tried to be the strong one and my rock. The Dr. sent me that night to go and get another methotrexate shot at the emergency room because in was late in the day. I waited there for four hours with a girlfriend on a Friday night. My husband was with my girlfriend's fiancé at their house. My girlfriend was so great to stay with me that long while a waiting to get the nasty shot that I was so dreading, not the shot but the drug. When we got back to my girlfriend's house my husband was noticeably upset and we went home. I had weaned myself off of the Lexapro because I was feeling better and I didn't want it in my system when I was trying to get pregnant again. Well of course, I had to start taking it again because of the depression. I took some time off of work the next week to deal with our loss. On Wednesday morning I went to get out of bed around 9:00 A.M. and it was like a light switch went off. I could not walk and could barely move because I was in so much excruciating pain. I called my husband as he was on his way to work and he said he would be there asap but had to go into the office for a few minutes to take care of something first. His job is an hour from our house. I knew I could not wait that long and need to go to the ER right then. I pretty much crawled into the bathroom and took a quick shower double over in pain, threw on some sweatpants and shirt, pulled my hair back, and had to at least put some powder and mascara on my face. I know that sounds crazy, but I never go out of the house without make up on. I didn't want to call an ambulance, but I know there was no way for me to drive. I called a couple friends and finally found one that was working from home that day and he said of course he would bring me. Once at the hospital, the nurses brought me right back to a room with the appropriate instruments to evaluate me, even though I knew what was going on. I couldn't help but scream and moan in pain. It was the worst pain I have ever experienced and I have broken many bones and been in bad car wrecks. This was so much worse. The nurses did not close the curtain and everyone in the ER was walking by and staring at me like I was a zoo animal or something. They gave me some dilaudid and that eased the pain and right then my husband walked and told me I would be alright. They took me back for surgery right after they confirmed that I had ruptured and was bleeding internally. My left tube was removed laparoscopically and I took 2 1/2 weeks off of work to recover phyisically and emotionally. My 37th birthday was on that Sunday after the operation. My sweet husband had planned a surprise birthday party for me with all of my closest friends. It was at a really nice restaurant that has a great brunch that I had been wanting check out. Needless to say, I did not feel like going at all. I felt like a bloated whale and was still sore from the laparoscopic surgery. He insisted that I needed to get out of the house, so I did. It was nice to see my very good friends and hear their empathy for both of us. I am glad that I did not sit home and sulk on my birthday thanks to my loving husband. Ten days after my next period I was schedule for an HSG. I read up on the procedure and was pretty frightened, so many horror stories about the pain. It wasn't bad at all and the good news was that my remaining right fallopian tube is open or patent. It is now July 2014 and my husband and I are trying to conceive again even though I am still an emotional mess. I think I cry on average 3-4 times a day. I am so very afraid that I will have another ectopic in my remaining left tube. If I do have another one, I am not sure what I should do. Should I have the Dr. take the tube and go the IVF route? Should I try and save the tube and try again? All I hear is the ticking of the clock in the back of my head. Each month that passess there is one less chance of us every having a family. My heart goes out to everyone that has experience infertility, it changes you to your very soul.

Melissa Charbonneau

It started as what I thought was a normal period; I had one the month before but this one seemed to go on forever. By the tenth day of bleeding I went to Planned Parenthood to get a checkup since my boyfriend and I aren't rolling in money. I was not in the examination room for 10 minutes before one of the nurses told me I was pregnant.

I could not really process the news because I knew bleeding and pregnancy don't really go well together and asked her to fetch my boyfriend from the waiting room. Once he sat down in the room, I told him I was pregnant and a huge smile went across his face that just melted my heart. We weren't trying but we weren't opposed to the idea of having a child.

Planned Parenthood suggested we go to the ER for ultrasounds immediately because of the bleeding. When we arrived they told me that I was 6-8 weeks along but could not find anything in the ultrasounds, both normal and transvaginal. They sent me away with Vicodin and said to follow up at our local ER in two days (as we were out of town when this occurred). All discharge information said "ectopic pregnancy ruled out".

When my boyfriend and I arrived back at our apartment in Seattle, we went to the local ER and had my blood tested. The hormone levels had dropped by nearly half and they told us we had miscarried. My boyfriend cried before I could even process the news. Again, we were sent home. Days later I began cramping terribly and had not yet stopped bleeding. It got to the point where I couldn't stand up straight and felt like I was going to pass out. I immediately went to the ER. I had blood drawn and was hooked to an iv for pain medication and fluids. I laid in a hospital for nearly 3 hours and finally had ultrasounds done. Hours later a doctor walked into my room and sat at the edge of my bed and told me I had an ectopic pregnancy and we needed to have surgery that evening. An hour later it was nearing 1am and I was being prepped for surgery. Terrified because my family and friends are back in Arizona, I only had my boyfriend to cry to. When I awoke from surgery my doctor told me that the pregnancy was almost 7cm and that there was over a liter of blood pooling in my stomach from the pregnancy.

Still fresh from the experience it has been about 20 days since my surgery. The bruising is dissipating and I am increasingly mobile. Nothing can explain how it felt to be told you have something so amazing and have it taken away. I cried when we were told we were miscarrying and have to this day. We hope to one day have a happy healthy child and that awareness of ectopic pregnancies rises. My thoughts go out to all who have gone through this terrible pain.

Randi age 26 my surgery was June 5, 2014 at 2am

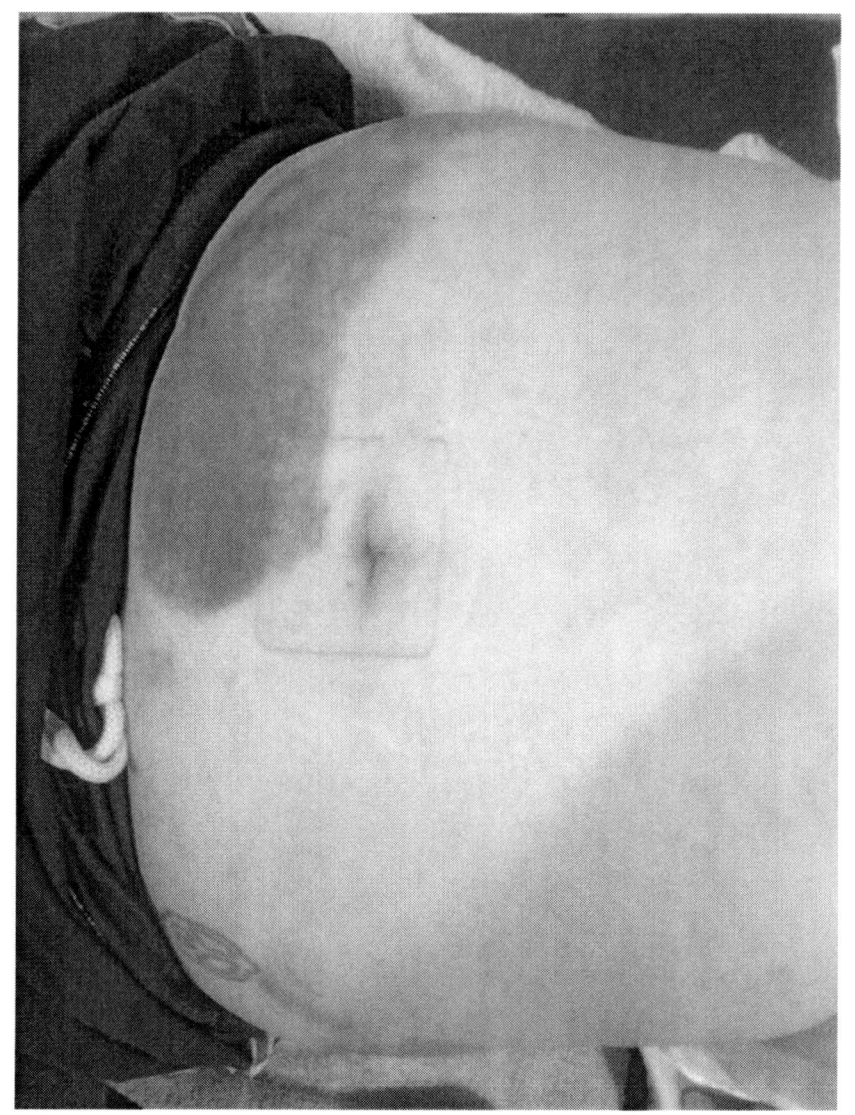

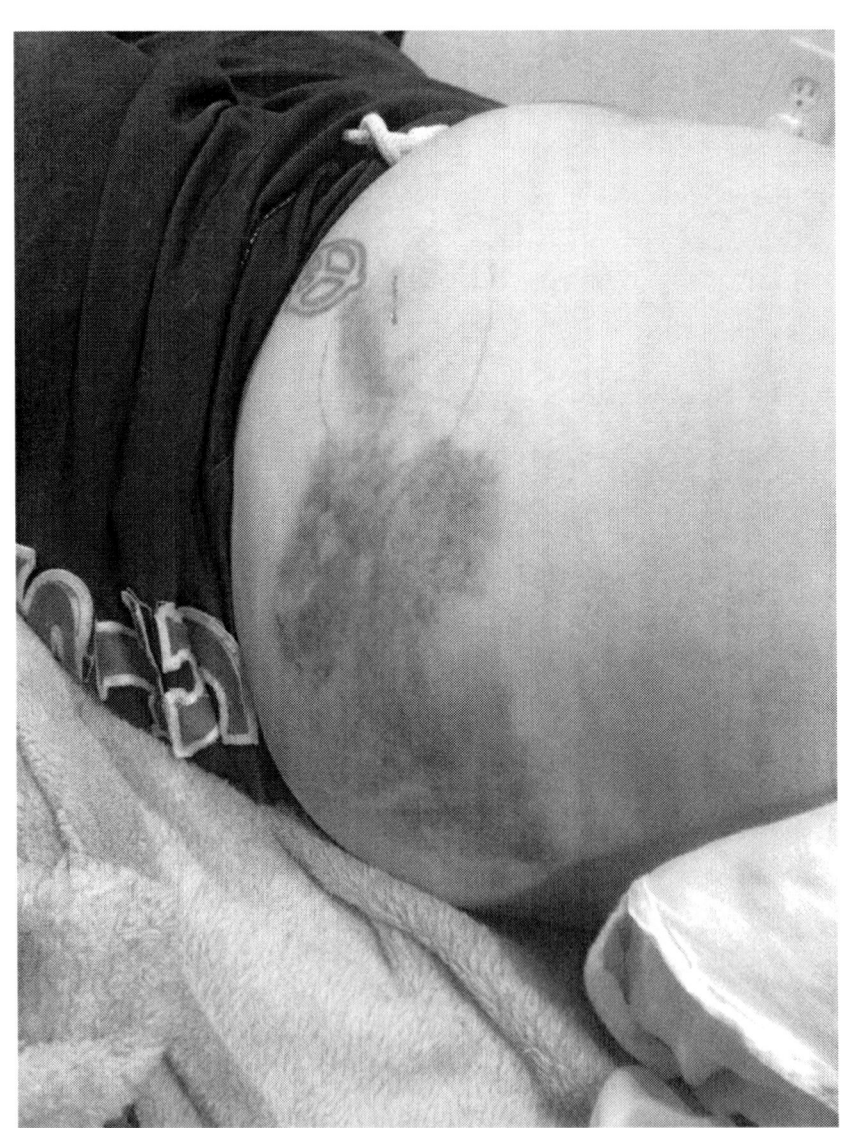

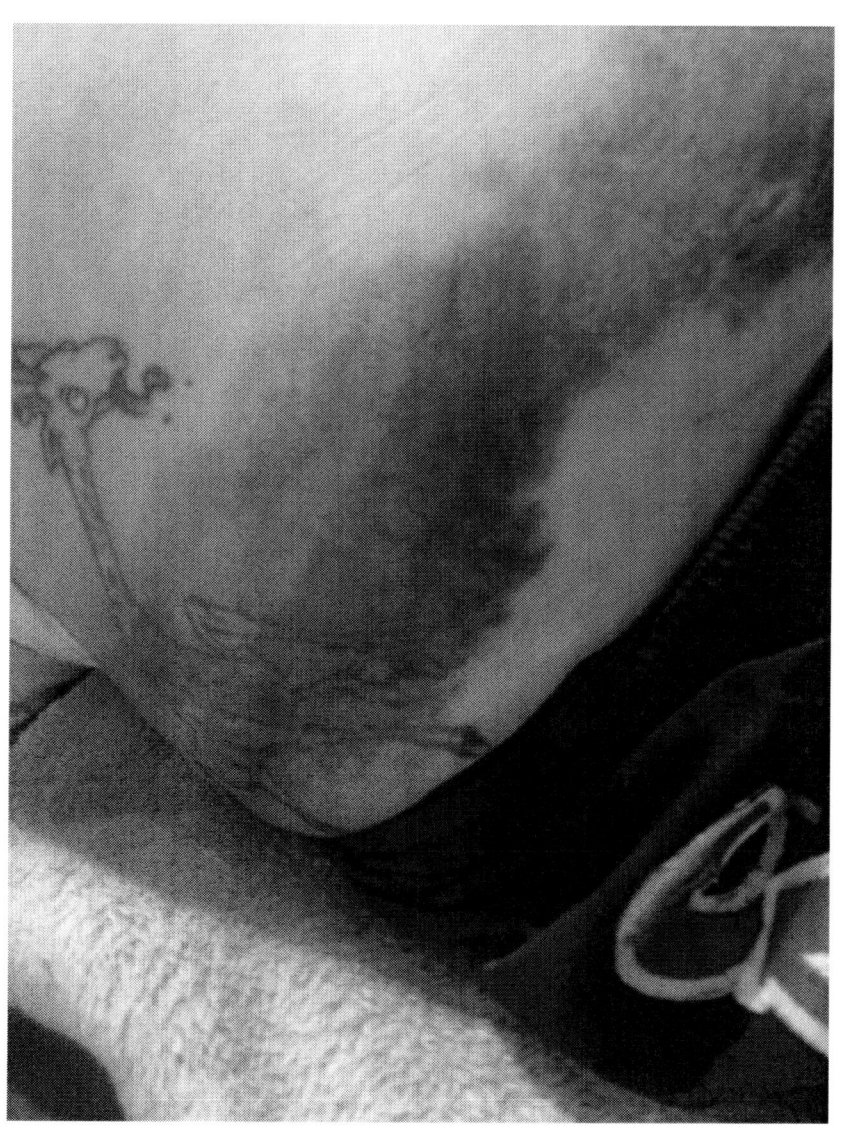

Randi

I was 24 years old. A day I thought was just like any other was a day that changed my life forever. On Jan. 23, 2012 on my dad's 8yr angelversary we went walking in our national park. At the same part we let my dad's ashes go I started feeling pain in my lower belly. Not thinking much of it we went on with the day. Later that night I started bleeding. So I decided to go to the hospital the next morning. We get to the hospital and they bring me to the back and start running test. They ask are you pregnant. And I say no not that I know of. So they did a test and we the nurse walks in and says well doctor she is pregnant. I got so happy and had to take a pic of the test. But then My heart dropped. And I realized. Wait why I am bleeding. Why do I feel this pain? What's wrong? They run more test and tell me I am 4-5 weeks pregnant. And that I may have an ectopic pregnancy. To go home relax and to return in 3 days for more test. As I went home we thought about names. We returned every 2-3 days for the next week or two. On Feb 1st I woke up feeling a little ill. As I lay on my mothers bed pail and dizzy she calls for help. I get rushed to the hospital. They ran test and kept me overnight. My numbers continue to rise as my baby continued to grow. As I layer in the hospital bed I began to pray for a sign. A sign on what my baby would be. As I prayed a lady walks in from my local church and ask me to pray with her. So I did. And she then hands me a blue rosary, but I loom at her arm with them and all she had was white and peach colored rosaries. Right then and there I knew god had given me a sign. That and in our hearts we felt our precious baby was going to be a boy. They then send me home once again. Knowing in my heart things were getting worse me and my husband decided to pick a name. We named our baby Johnny Torres. On Feb 11th as I walk into my kitchen I stop and freeze. The pain hit so bad I could not move. As I lay there waiting for ems to come my nephew with us and he was so concerned. They rush me to the hospital and they run test. They confirm my tube ruptured and I needed emergency surgery. As I lay in that hospital bed once again a tear falls. My baby is gone. That was the most horrible day I could ever have felt. A piece of us died that day and we will never get it back. In our hearts our baby boy Johnny will forever be until we meet again. All we have for our baby is my surgery scar, a picture of a pregnancy test and our broken hearts.
Fly high Johnny, but forever live on in our hearts
    In Memory of
    Johnny Torres
        2/11/12
I own a Facebook page called Precious Angel Beading. I make beaded ribbons, bracelets, and necklaces in memory of angel babies gone to soon.
www.Facebook.com/preciousangelbeading

Christina Torres

My wife (33) and I (23) started trying for our first baby in Nov 2013. In February 2014 I started bleeding/spotting around the time of ovulation that lasted a week or so, I decided to do a pregnancy test and it came back positive! I could not believe it I could barely breath and I was shaking I had never been happier. I put the pregnancy test in my wife's anniversary card as it was the next day and I wanted it to be a surprise but I couldn't wait so I gave it to her that night (16/2/14) we could not wipe the smiles off our faces. We thought it was going to take forever as we where doing home insemination. We went to the doctors to get it confirmed and because I was starting to worry about the bleeding I had. We had to wait a day for a ultrasound, had the ultrasound and they couldn't find our baby, We where both in tears. He said he could see blood that shouldn't be there and wanted to check my tubes, he did an internal ultra sound and as soon as he did that I almost screamed from the pain he sent us straight back to the dr. The Dr said it was ectopic, that we had conceived in December 2013 and we where 9-10 weeks, he wrote us a letter and told us to go straight to hospital. It all happened so quickly. I was rushed in and before I had time for it to sink in I was getting prepped for surgery. The surgeon told me my tube had ruptured and they had to remove my tube and I was loosing blood fast and would I accept blood. I balled my eyes out as soon as they took me into the surgery waiting part and told my wife that she couldn't come any further. I tried to be so strong for her the whole time. I was put under still crying. I woke up and I was hoping it was all just a horrible night mare but it wasn't. I nearly died and we had just lost our first baby. I felt so empty and my heart was broken. They finally took me to the ward and my wife was waiting for me. We both broke down in tears and cried for ages. We both where shattered and just destroyed. We both didn't realize just how hard it was loosing a baby. The surgeon showed us photos from my operation which was very confronting; it was such an emotional roller coaster. I kept wondering why us, why did it happen and blaming myself. The next few weeks where so hard I would just burst into tears all the time. I would have to ring councilors twice a week or more to help with how I was feeling and to try get out of the bad head space I was in. My wife and I got a teddy bear made up for our baby we lost that we could always cuddle and look at and remember our beautiful angel baby not that we would ever forget. I couldn't even look at photos of little kids on Facebook or be around them, I went into a bad depression. Even Months after it's still so hard and heart breaking, I'm starting to have more good days than bad. I found support groups on line for ectopics and they helped so much and been able to talk about it as much as I needed was a huge help and to know that we weren't alone. We are now currently trying for another baby which has been quite emotional but know our angel baby is always in our hearts and will be looking over his or hers brother or sister. It is such a hard thing to go threw, there is light at the end of the tunnel.

Anonymous

My name is Danielle Tafoya I'm 18 years old. On march 8, 2014 I took like 7 test and it finally hit me that I was pregnant... A week later I wasn't feeling right so my boyfriend took me to the ER (I was about 5 or 6 weeks) I had slight cramping and bleeding off and on.... They did an ultrasound but couldn't find anything saying it was just too early yet. An hour later they came back and said turns out I was in the process of a miscarriage and sent me home to let nature take its course and come back on Sunday. The next day I was resting at home when the pain shifted to my right side and I had a fever of 101. We went to a diff hospital to where they ran a million other tests. They came back saying my hcg levels were still rising but not like they should be they came back half an hour layer stating I had a busted cyst which caused all the pain and bleeding. Although they still said I could be having a miscarriage. Here I am going crazy so I have to wait 2 WEEKS till my next ultrasound!!! During those two weeks I was crawling the walls going crazy because even though they said I miscarried every blood test I had still said I was pregnant and every pee test I bought said it too. Finally the day of my ultrasound 3/28/14. We go and get it an hour later I get a call from my Dr directly and she tells me that I need to get to the hospital and check in that they already have a room for me. Turns out I have an eptopic pregnancy. An hour later we get to the hospital half an hour later they admitted me an hour later I was prepped for emergency surgery... An hour and a half later there are no longer two heartbeats in me but only one... The next day the Dr tells me that if they waited an extra day I could've died. On top of now I no longer have a left tube either. I was 9 weeks. We didn't know the sex but we always dream of a girl. We named her Morgan meaning free spirit of the sea and protected of the sea creatures. I didn't get my ultrasound pic because they didn't give me one the only photos i have are these please don't judge or laugh :,(I wish I had more pictures! I wish i still had my test... But out of anger I threw them and tore down her little clothes holder in my closet with all her bibs and onsies I bought her.

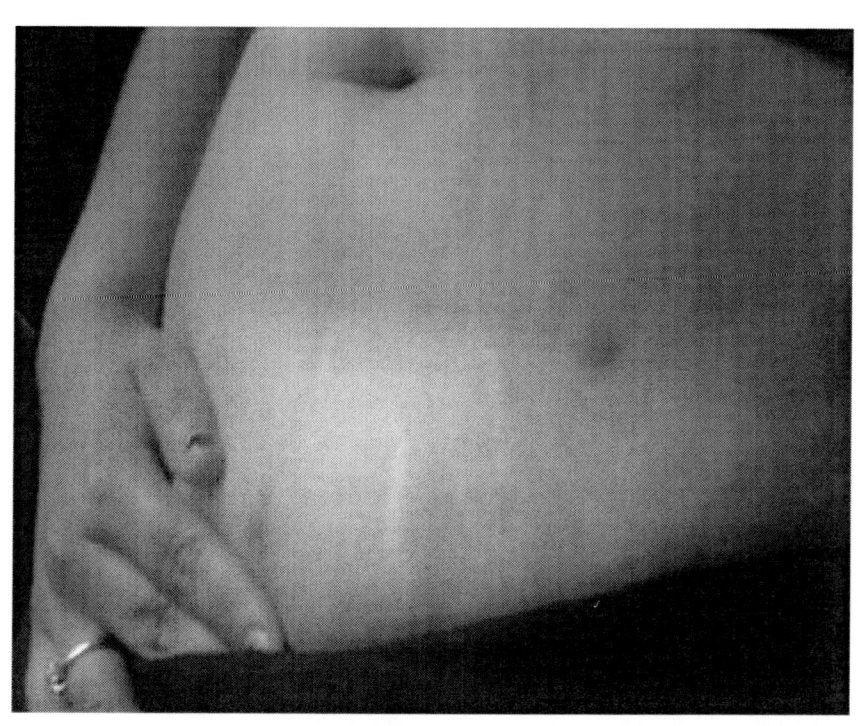

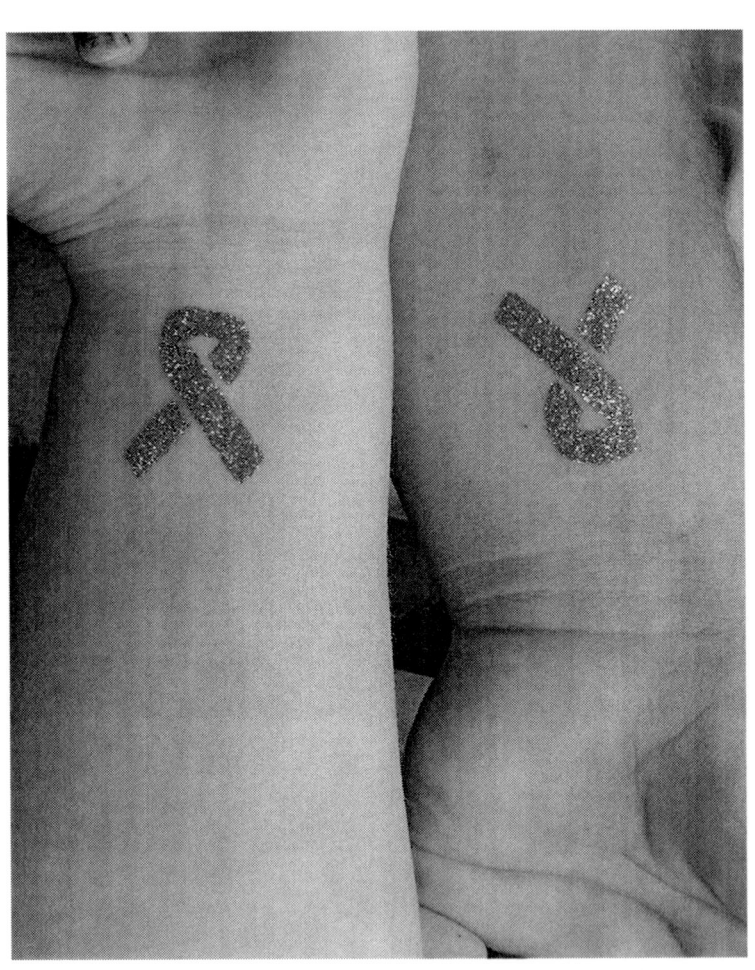

Danielle Tafoya

My name is Carey Hathaway. My husband and I were married in the spring of 2000. We had lived together for two years prior to being married. I became pregnant during our first year together. I had an ectopic pregnancy. I found out after having hernia surgery because, upon my return back to work, the very first night back, I was in so much pain that I couldn't bear it. I was taken to the hospital, and that's when I found out that I was pregnant, but that it was ectopic. I had no idea what that meant at the time. I learned very fast. After that, we were married. We decided to do invitro a year or so after that. We fertilized six eggs and used three the first time and froze the rest. It didn't work. We decided since it really didn't cost that much once you already had frozen embryos to do it again. We tried once more with no success. We've always wanted children of our own, we thought about adoption, but we exhausted all of our funds. Adoption is really expensive. My husband is such a kind and caring man, he would be such a good father. It makes me so sad that we can't have children. Upon doing invitro, they took my other Fallopian tube, it had some fluid in it. They said if I were to get pregnant that it would be an unhealthy environment for an embryo. I feel for anyone who can't have children. They are such a blessing. This is my story...I hope that it can ease someone else's pain. I know what it's like to see a sweet baby, hear children laughing, or watching them sleep like angels knowing that it will never happen for you. There are so many people that are mean to children, or who don't want them. All that I can say is, they will have to answer one day for what they have done with what they were given. Thanks for letting me share.

Carey Hathaway

A lot of the posts that I have seen on your page seem to come from older woman, so I thought I'd share my story for all the young mothers out there. I wish I could give you my story in detail but it would be way too much.

I am a 22 year old, with the pressure of my family pushing me to towards success. I happened to be that one family member whose every move is monitored, the one to make all the "right" decisions in life.

About 3 weeks ago, I had discovered that I had been having an ectopic pregnancy which had ruptured my left Fallopian tube. I was then told I needed emergency surgery and my tube was to be removed. I had no medical insurance or hospital plan and the surgeon who operated on me only knew about my case 2 hours before the surgery.

Indeed this was the most frightening experience in my life and I had to go through it all on my own. Don't get me wrong, my family and boyfriend supported me all the way, but the only time I got to see them was 2 hours in a day. To add to the drama I was told that there had been something in my uterus, possibly another fertilized egg. A different doctor discharged me the next day, and I questioned the "existing egg". The only answer received was that I need to take another test in a month's time to see if the existing egg survived the surgery. It's all been frustrating to the point where I just take it one day at a time and let it be...

Now I can write long essays about my experience and how traumatic it was, but none of it compares to the thought of losing a child.

My biggest fear was not being able to have kids one day, I know that I am young and have a whole life ahead of me, but I've realized that there is more to life than money and material possessions.

Every night lay in bed and cry questioning why me? I wonder how different things would have been. It's been two weeks later and no one has asked me how feel, it's just expected of me to forget it all.

My heart goes out to all ectopic survivors, mothers who had lost a baby and those who experienced miscarriage. I thought I was alone, but there are so many woman out there just like me...

-Ashleigh T

I'm 22 and in September I went through my first eptopic I was having pains but choice to ignore them I went to my 12 week scan and was told there was nothing there I had a internal can and they found a eptopic on my left tube I was rushed to theatre for a emergency operation when I woke up they told me that my tube had just ruptured they burnt the hole instead of taking the tube In January I found out I was pregnant and booked up for a 6 week scan 2 day before the scan I suffered a miscarriage

In April I found out I was pregnant again I was so scared I packed my hospital bag just incase I went for my 6 week scan but this time they could see something on my left side right side and in my womb I had to have blood tests and internal scans every other day to see if anything had changed after a week and half of this they decided to take me to theatre to find out what was going on I was ready for surgery and waited 12 hours and was told that I would have to wait till the following day after surgery the doctors came to see me as soon as I woke up I was told I had a eptopic in my right side this time a lump of skin growth on my left where it had healed that they had removed my my left tube is very damaged and the shadow in the womb was a fake pregnancy that can happen with eptopic pregnancy I have been told to wait a year then give it a year of trying but if I don't fall pregnant my left tube isn't working but I was also told if I do get pregnant there is over 50% chance I will have a eptopic again that will leave me with no tubes I have already got a four year old little girl so wouldn't be able to get any help with ivf

Anonymous

I have a story to tell I am a 25 yrs old young lady who has 1 daughter (4) by C-section born 2010.29.08.... My 1st ectopic was in 2012 in July 3 I had been pregnant since January 2012 but never noticed since I was going on my periods, one day (July 2 2012) I got really sick turned pale n couldn't walk I was rushed to hospital and found out I had an ectopic pregnancy that was tragic 4 me since I want to have a big family and I love kids to death... So that was it but I never stopped yearning for another child, I stopped taken contraceptives a month after the ectopic and hoped that I will fall pregnant and my boyfriend was always talking about the baby we lost adding to my depression he even named him Duncan. Towards the end of Oct 2012 my left leg started reacting now and then I popped pain killers and moved on with my life and pain got server in November so I took a pregnancy test it showed as Invalid. At the beginning of December 2012 I had 1 rough night and I could not sleep the left leg was killing me so the next morning I was rushed to the clinic by my boyfriend and when I got there they called an ambulance I had to undergo another operation since I was having an Ectopic pregnancy again... Months later I thought of taking my life and sometimes I still do but when I look in my only daughter's eyes I see a reason to embrace life. I wish I could have more children and when I was in my teen years and asked by other girls how many children would you like to have I always said 13 lol. I come from a large family and my grandmother gave birth to 10 children and the fact that I will only have 1 child just breaks my heart

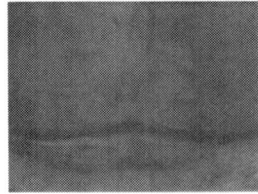

Nomcebo Ngema

I'm 21 with a little boy. First started on Friday the 2nd of May. My little boy was in daycare and I was trying to fill in time driving around town looking at the shops due to living out of town at that time and only having one car. I started spotting and getting pains but just thought it was my period. Was coming and going so didn't think much of it's by that night the bleeding had stopped. Woke up Saturday morning and could hardly move I stood up and had blood just run down my leg like urine but I had to get up to look after my son while my partner was at work.. So had a shower which helped a little. By 10am I was on the phone crying to him I had been bleeding heavy and was getting contraction like pains again which put me in tears on the floor. He couldn't come home and by the time he got home later that day at 1pm the pain had eased. Early Sunday morning I woke up to contraction like pains again. Woke up in the morning to my son and wasn't hurting as much so told my partner I didn't need to go to the hospital then the pain again. We dropped bub off to his sister and off for the hour drive to the hospital. Got to emergency and they did obs and put me straight into a small room with a bed that said gyno on the door. Looked at my partner and said this doesn't look good. Was given a dose of morphine after being there for about 10mins. Was still in heaps of pain so after about 20mins I was given another dose after that I'm not real sure on details I was pretty out of it but my partner filled me in. I was given blood tests between morphine and the nurse had come back and told me I was pregnant and that they were sending me for an ultrasound. The ultrasound was done and the lady said she was unsure but could see a mass and fluid. I was put back in the room and then another dose of morphine because of the pain. I didn't know how to feel also don't think it really sunk in. The Dr come in and was talking to me asking questions and said that they could see a mass and fluid but he was going to leave me for the night and see how I went but wanted to check with his boss to be sure..

He left not sure for how long and come back saying that I was going in for the op he wasn't sure what they were going to do until he got in there.. But I had to wait for a little girl to have her appendix out. I was prepped and waited. The pushed me to the doors of the recovery unit where my partner had to leave me. Was in there for what felt like ages before I was wheeled Into the theatre. Woke up in recovery not knowing where a was to a face I didn't know but she was nice and gave me an ice block. I can't remember much but was told as I was being wheeled to my room my partner kissed me and gave me flowers and a teddy. He told me he was talking to me and the nurses checked my blood pressure and then again they even got another machine until one told my partner she was going to press a button and heaps of des would be there in minutes. It was the emergency button my blood pressure had dropped he said he was so scared he stepped back enough so that if I looked around I could still see him.. He thought they were going to wheel me back to theatre. He had also heard that I had lost 200mls or more of blood. I had a really nice nurse to help me though after my partner left.. In the morning I waiting for my partner to get into town the Dr come to talk to me.. He told me that I had an eptopic pregnancy and my tube had ruptured so they had to remove it. He showed me photos from the op and said I could go home and just needed to see my gp in 2weeks that was all fine. Until I got a call on Friday the 9th so just under a week later saying I needed to go into the epac (early pregnancy assessment centre) on the Monday at 830am I didn't know what to think. It was only for bloods to see if my hcg had gone down but wasn't told anything. All come back clear. The ultrasound was inconclusive but they think I was about 6weeks. And was named baby Tattersal

Anonymous

I'm 29 years old and from Brisbane Australia. Me and my husband, also 29 have been trying for 6 years to conceive. I have a health issues. I am very low on Iron, as in I constantly bleed. No one since I was 16 years old has been able to help me or figure where or why this is happening. On the 5th of July 2013, I had my very first Laparoscopy at the Royal Brisbane Hospital to see what was going on inside. 6 weeks later for my check up, they said it all looked fine. He wasn't sure about my bleeding and then he prescribed me to the contraceptive pill to try regulate things. I stayed on the pill for 4 months until I decided to stop because I was moody and depressed, gained weight and just unhappy. In November last year I also started acupuncture and had been back 3 times after. Through Christmas and New Years of this year, 2014, I was still bleeding/spotting so nothing was different for me. The morning of the 11th February 2014 at 3am I was getting ready for work but could hardly stand. I had this sharp intense pain in my lower right ovary area and my lower right back. My husband then took me to the local hospital and they did tests and an ultra sound/pelvic scan and a couple hours later told me I had a cyst on my right ovary-which I already knew about. So they gave me pain relief pills for 10 hours as they watched over me and then I was sent home. The following morning I was in worse pain, I had never felt this pain before. So my husband rushed me back to the hospital, the ED nurse came in and said to us "well do you think it has anything to do with your pregnancy?" We were shocked and I just burst into tears and said "what do you mean?" He then apologized and said he would go away and read my report from the day before. A couple minutes past that felt like a life time for us and he returned and apologized to us saying he was surprised no one had told us the day before that our urine sample came up with a positive pregnancy test and our blood showed pregnant. He then said because they couldn't see anything the day before in my pelvic scans that it was highly an Ectopic. The Gynecologist came down and explained to me that we were pregnant, that our baby was stuck in a place it would not survive and that it is very dangerous for me. So all within 20mins I found out I was pregnant and then rushed to surgery to have it removed. Through the procedure I did lose my right fallopian tube. Since February of this year I've had irregular bleeding, so its been hard trying to be intimate to even try again for a baby. We just had our IVF appointment on the 7th of this month, July and they said they cant help me until my bleeding is controlled and investigated further. So now it's the waiting game to see the specialist.

This is my story

Elisa

Hi my name is Jodie this pass June has made 2 years since I had my ectopic pregnancy and lost my right tube and my little angel I was filling sick so I went to the ER and turns out I was pregnant and I starting freaking out because I was on the birth control mirena and knew something could happen to my baby so an hour later a nurse comes back in and tells me it's a ectopic pregnancy and I needed surgery and my baby wouldn't make it. I had my surgery the next day I have 3 scars across my belly now never got to see, touch, fill nothing of my baby and now since I only have one tube my Dr says its going be really hard to have another baby well that's my story

Signed Jodie Charlie Desormeaux

Hi I have had 2 ectopic pregnancies but 3 surgeries. In 2009 I found out I was pregnant but having not have been with my current partner for a long time it was very unexpected. I went through every emotion and dare I say it.. Not too sure if it was what id actually wanted? 8 weeks pregnant. I had sudden pain in my right side. Thought maybe was wind etc? So I called the docs after being examined, sent to hospital and then confirmed by ultrasound I was indeed having an ectopic pregnancy I was so upset. I felt so guilty that I'd even questioned this baby and felt like it was my punishment that it was being taken away from me. I had to have emergency surgery as my tube ruptured and I was internally bleeding. I was told I was lucky to be alive. I had to leave that hospital tired, drained, without my little seed Billie (baby) and also missing my right tube! I did then go on to have my gorgeous girl 11 months later. If it wasn't for our little Billie our precious daughter probably wouldn't have been conceived!?? Again in Feb. 2014 for a few days suffered nigly shoulder pain? One morning though my left side was agony o struggled to drive my kids to school. Surely not another ectopic. I had the merena coil so surely I was safe? Immediately my friend got me a pregnancy test and yes it confirmed I was indeed pregnant. I called the gp surgery and explained the situation also i was in agony but they couldn't see me for another 7 hours??! So straight to a+e I went! Within 4 hours I was severely ill and taken for emergency surgery once again as my left tube had ruptured and I had blood leaking into my tummy. Nurses told me I was very lucky to be here and if i had waited till 5:30 to see my gp I may not have been here telling this story now!! The surgeon tried his best to save my tube as I am only 29 yrs and its my last one. I got home day after surgery!! This was all so sudden!? I had to get my hcg levels tested every week to make sure no cells were left. After 2 weeks I felt like I was getting back to normal until.. I received a phone call from the hospital telling me I had to go back in as my hcg levels were double what they were at very beginning, even before the surgery!? How can that be? What did they take out in surgery then if my baby was still growing inside me? I had to then go for more surgery to remove my left tube too as it was now damaged again. I left that hospital drained emotionally and mentally. I know I already have my beautiful kiddies but now I can't have anymore!? It's just not fair!! All my little girl says she wants to when she's older is a big sister. It's heartbreaking!! Me and my partner weren't ready to give up having more babies! Its not fair that now we don't have a choice and I cant help bit think maybe of the job was done right with first op in 2014 we may still have had the slightest bit chance left of having more babies?? I am learning now to deal with it better. Its sometimes really hard when people don't understand they just think..."oh well it wasn't a baby yet anyway" but yes it was it was mine!! And now I have nothing!.. Nothing but a whole that I can't even replace as I have also had that privilege taken away from me too. Hoping that one day it will get easier!?

From Lee-Ashley Graham

20year old usually healthy, happily in a stable relationship March 11th 2014 was the day I lost my baby and almost lost my life..... Previously to this date I had been to the doctors for pregnancy test came back negative.... I then had a small period which I thought was normal few days after the bleeding I started feeling tired, eating a lot and felt pregnant so I took a home pregnancy test came back positive we were over the moon! Couldn't have been any happier that we were going to become parents 6weeks into my pregnancy on the 10 march I was feeling more tired than normal so had an early night and went to bed around 12oclock I made a phone to nhs 24 with severe pain in my stomach, passing out , fever I explained I was pregnant but the lady insisted it was only a stomach bug told me to get some sleep and drink plenty of water by morning I couldn't move for the sharp pain shooting through my stomach so I called 999 who rushed me to a&e ending up with emergency key hole surgery removing my left Fallopian tube and 2ltr of blood, I spent a week in hospital getting blood transfusions , antibiotics after discharged from hospital a week later I was still having severe stomach pain so a trip to the doctors I went who transferred me to the hospital where I had another key hole surgery to remove a further 500ml of blood, after having this scary experience and being told I almost lost my life has scared me for sure....

Anonymous

So my story starts after I had my tubes tied for about 2 years and I was late and having some pains. I took 2 tests and they were barely visible but to me it seemed positive, I called the Drs Office and got in a couple days later on a Monday. The Dr didn't seem to be paying attention, when she first walked in she didn't even have my file. When I told her what was going on she didn't look at the tests that I brought, she told me the test they took came back negative and that it seemed like I wanted to be pregnant. I left thinking I was fine and it was in my head. 4 days later on September 6th out of no where I started having this horrible pain on my lower left side. That night it got so bad I couldn't even pee. My husband had to call 911 to take me to the hospital. After I got there they took some blood and gave me an IV so I could pee. After about 30-45 minutes the nurse asked me if there was any way I could be pregnant and I told her no my tubes were tied and my Dr had said no just the other day. She then told me that my test came back positive, I lost it. I started crying and telling her it couldn't be. By that time it was around midnight and 6/7/13, they told me I was going to have an ultrasound to find where the baby was and how far along I was. The ultrasound tech could only find out how far along I was and she said I was 6 weeks. After she was done, they prepped me for surgery. I called my mom so she could come up and help calm me down. After I had woken up I was told the baby was in my left tube and they had to remove it and a cup of blood. Till this day I still have nightmares and there is not a day that goes by that I'm not thinking of my angel.

Felicia Schattilly

Wow amazing blue line on the test myself and now ex was over the moon the line was only faint

but was there, we made an appointment for the following week to get it confirmed I went through

all the morning sickness and then started to bleed so made an earlier appointment only to be told

that by the sounds I was miscarrying they arranged an appointment at the epau unit for 2 days

later a very anxious time for us both sleepless nights worrying tears shed was walking around in a

zombified manor tbh, gets to the epau where I had blood tests done and then they told me that I

would be having a scan ASAP to see if it had come away or whether it was just a bleed as the

test was still positive, laid shaking waiting for the scan the cold jelly went on my belly and I let

myself for a flicker of what seemed like a second of pure excitement would be seen on the screen

any minute now for the scan lady to say can you stay there whilst I get someone else to come

and have a look, myself and my partner at the time looked at each other with pure dread, the

other person came in commenced with the scan then turned to us to tell us I am sorry to tell you

this but you are having an ectopic pregnancy and it will need to be removed ASAP so we are

going to take you down to theatre, I didn't even get the chance to come to terms with it I was only

allowed to make a couple of quick phone calls so that childcare arrangements could be made for

my two eldest children, I was taken straight into theatre and the operation commenced when I

come round from the operation one of the nurses said to me as I was drugged up with painkillers

the operation was a success I just looked at her and thought SUCESS I have just lost a baby

yeah it isn't born yet but it was still my baby that I had carried for 6 weeks and 3 days they told

me. when I was receiving the aftercare the doctor told me that they had managed to save half of

my left fallopian tube and would / should have no problem conceiving again... like that is what

was on my mind at that time and I was sent home with bruises all over and strong painkillers and

told to rest life just seemed to float on by for the next few weeks days merged into nights and

nights merged into days I was just like a robot fully grief stricken. six months later I went to brush

my teeth as normal in the morning and I felt a sudden wave of sickness and I said to my partner at the time I think I need to do a test so he went and got me a test from the local chemist erging me to do it straight away but I couldn't bring myself to do it till the next day when the same wave of sickness overcome me I did the test and left it on the side and carried out normal household chores for ten minutes and then went back to look at the test as my partner didn't want to do it I looked and then walked away thinking that I had read it as a negative about an hour later the stick was still on the side when I needed the toilet I sat on the toilet and for some reason I picked up the stick and held it there staring at it there was a very faint blue line a shock of fear and excitement came around me as I shouted my partner I showed him the stick he took me in his arms and smiled as I broke down in tears fearing that I would experience the same again, we made an appointment to have it confirmed at the doctors which was still a very faint line by this time and they put it down to being very early on in the pregnancy so we left, a few days later I experienced stomach pains and blood loss again this time to be seen by a nurse who's words was if your miscarrying your miscarrying there is nothing I can do!, I was devastated and we went home where I wasn't allowed to do anything as all the family thought rest would help the situation for a couple more days I had excruciating pain and was finally referred back to the epau because of my previous where the scans showed nothing they could see I was pregnant but couldn't find the baby only to be told I was either to early for the scan to pick up or there was something going on with the hormone levels in my blood and I had already miscarried I had to go back and forth to the hospital for checkups every day for 8 days for them to still not find anything on scans but my pregnancy hormone was rising but at a very slow rate slower than most pregnant women at this point we had known I was pregnant for just over 2 and a half weeks, before the last scan I had the doctor had said to us in the morning you could possibly be expecting twins with your hormone levels being the way they are but we just cant see them on the scan so they must be tiny bearing in mind I am only 4ft9 anyway and my partner was only just over 5ft , I had a scan and still nothing was seen so we sat with the consultant to be given an option of having a tablet to abort the pregnancy voluntarily as they could not understand what was happening my mind was just numb I didn't know how to feel how to react or anything I asked if I could go home to think about it and they told me no as I needed the procedure ASAP and would need to be weighed and examined thoroughly before the tablet I went outside for some fresh air with my partner whilst I gathered my thoughts together on the way back up to the ward after deciding very heartbrokenly that I would have the tablet but didn't want to I experienced the most excruciating pain imaginable my partner had to literally carry me back to the ward as there was no help around I said I need the toilet only to bend over and the pain got more and more immense so was laid on a bed on the ward in a side room where I was told I would be taken down to theatre and they would investigate what was happening after four nurses 2 of which was students tried to put a canula in as my veins were collapsing I was eventually wheeled down to theatre which seemed like a lifetime of waiting. coming round back on the ward I could hear my partner talking to one of the nurses saying please let me tell her as it will be better if it comes from me at this time it was early hours the next morning they agreed and then told him that he had to go home and come back for visiting hours the day after he came and sat on the edge of the bed tears down his face and looked gray when he said to me it happened again but they have removed all of your right tube, I was then left alone to deal with this heartbreaking news I cried myself to an awoken sleep the next day a surgeon came to see me apparently he was a big man that had to be rushed in from another hospital he sat at the side of me and told me that he was called in as they found I was heavily bleeding but couldn't see where from I had actually ruptured and if I had been left much longer I could of died he then went on to tell me that I would have been around 8 weeks and 2 days into the pregnancy and that whilst he was stopping the bleed he looked at my left hand tube where I had had the previous ectopic to be told that they had in fact removed that tube on my first operation and my right tube was in a state of no repair so that had to be removed as well I was now classed as being fully infertile I would never experience pregnancy again unless I went forward for ivf. I was in a state of disbelief totally bruised, heartbroken, grief-stricken you name it I felt it even self blame was felt I was a woman but no longer felt that way women are here to conceive and reproduce these are the worst feelings in the world and every month I have a period and what for?? my only thing that I remember when each period occurs is that I can never have another child and this has been how I have felt ever since, a baby was growing inside me and never made it to the outside world but for that brief time my babies had inside me was filled with love even though it was a scary love especially with the second ectopic but they still exists in my heart and thoughts to this very day the grief has got slightly easier but there is never a day that I forget them and I have a scar on each side of my bellybutton for reminders as well they were my babies and always will be

SARA ROBBINS

On Easter Sunday, my husband & I were excited to find out that we were expecting our 4th child. We have 3 boys, so we wanted to give it one last shot for a girl. On that following Friday I started to bleed, I was devastated. I went to my appointment that I had already scheduled for that Monday, only to be told that it was probably an early miscarriage. I continued for several days to have symptoms, so I called to make another appointment, but before I could make it I ended up in the ER in terrible pain. The ER preformed an ultrasound, but didn't see anything but a huge cyst on my left ovary. They told me that's more than likely what was causing my pain. I seen my doctor the next day who said that he would monitor my HCG levels & do an ultrasound once a week until we had some sort of answer as to why I was hurting & bleeding. Three days later the pain had gotten so bad I couldn't stand it & I started to bleed black blood. My doctor told me to rush to the ER where they decided to perform emergency surgery. The baby was in my left tube, so he had to remove my tube & also ended up removing my left ovary. I was in surgery for almost 3 hours. My recovery was difficult, but more than anything it has been very heartbreaking. Thank you for giving me the opportunity to share my story.

-Autumn Waldroup

Well here goes the first time I've ever actually talked about my baby because people don't understand they say get over it move on it wasn't meant to be but I will never stop hurting for my baby. Well found out I was pregnant almost 2yr ago I was so happy but was bleeding went to the doctor who sent me for a emergency scan my partner couldn't make it as he was working but I wasn't scarred I really did believe everything was going to b ok but I was so wrong my baby wasn't in the rite place he didn't make his journey to my womb where I could keep him safe he safe he got stuck in my left tube when I looked at that screen I didn't believe what the doctor was telling me my baby still had a heartbeat and was still growing fighting 9wk4days I will never get that image out of my head I just wish his dad was there maybe he would of understood if he seen but he didn't I felt so alone he didn't even take time of work he left me to deal with it all alone that night I got admitted ready for surgery the next morning I begged them not to take my baby away that night was the worst I cried all night the thought of them taking a part of me I dreamt that night of my baby and I still have it often I can see my baby but can't hold him he is crying and it kills me I wake crying most nights but anyway after surgery I went home to a empty house my partner was working and my son who was one at the time was staying with grandparents I didn't get to see my son for over a week till I recovered the days get easier but I still think about my baby everyday it will be 2 year on the 25th July I'm dreading it as I also lost a baby 7 month ago just to think if life was how it was meant to be id have a 3 yr old and almost 2 yr old and I'd b feeling my baby kick and move and be getting ready for he/she to enter the world but that wasn't my destiny I feel blessed for my little boy and will cherish him forever but will never forget about my 2 angel babies

Anonymous

Feb 2013 - We hadn't really been trying for a baby but weren't using precautions either, I was

sitting having a cup of tea with my mother late in the evening when I felt a shooting pain in my

boobs which I thought strange, when I thought about it I then realized I was 3 days late, my

period hadn't arrived and no sign of it coming so the next morning I went to get a home

pregnancy test, it came up positive straight away, I did a few more to be sure and all were

positive, my partner and I were so excited,

I had slight cramps which I thought were normal, almost like constipation pain so I started taking

prunes which helped a little but the pain was still there, it wasn't so uncomfortable that It worried

me so I put it to the back of my mind, I attended the doctor 2 days later to confirm the pregnancy

and to my horror the test came back negative, it was almost like somebody tore my heart out, she

told me to come back a few days later to repeat, I went home and bought a Clearblue digital test

which showed pregnant 3-4 weeks, by my dates I was 5 weeks and 1 day pregnant, I went for the

repeat test in doctors office 3 days later and pregnancy test was positive so I rang hospital to

book my first appointment which was 6 weeks later, 2 days later the horror began, I felt

something wet on my underwear, it was brown blood, I was so upset, the next day I went to ER,

the scan showed no baby in uterus and I was told to return the following day to Epu as I had

either already miscarried or was having an ectopic pregnancy, I didn't know much about ectopic

pregnancy at the time and I remember goggling it and thinking I'm having one of these I just knew

in my heart, next morning I attended as instructed, I was given an internal u/s which I remember

being very uncomfortable, the rest all happened so fast, doctor seen baby in my left tube and

looked worried, I was told I would need emergency surgery, I was devastated and crying

uncontrollably, I was brought to the ward and prepared for surgery when the same lady doctor

came to see me said I may not need surgery after and may be able to have an injection instead

all as my hcg levels were very low,

She made a decision to watch and wait, 48 hours later I had repeat blood test and levels had

dropped again so she was happy nature was taking its course, I was released from hospital and given a follow up appointment 3 days later at which stage my levels were only 5 so I was definitely losing the baby myself and I was discharged from outpatients and told if I get pregnant

again I would need to be seen at 6 weeks

August 2013 - I had just came off birth control and the following month my period was late, I decided to wait 5 days before testing,

Test day came and I was terrified, I found the courage and straight away it was positive, I was so scared and would not allow myself to get excited, I rang the hospital and they said I could be seen at 7 weeks which didn't seem too long, my partner was off work on Mondays so I arranged an appointment so he could come with me to the ultrasound, I would have been 8 weeks 1 day by that stage, I had no pain or bleeding so was starting to get excited as the scan day approached,

It was the Thursday beforehand and I started to have bad diarrhea which was followed by vomiting, I rang the ER and was told it was probably a vomiting bug and to drink lots of fluids to keep hydrated, I felt very weak and collapsed on the floor a while later, the process repeated itself so an ambulance was called, at this stage I was in terrible pain all over my stomach, the paramedics thought my appendix had burst so I was brought to the nearest hospital where it was confirmed in was having another ectopic pregnancy, I was in so much pain and the doctor fitted a catheter as I was unable to get out of bed, I was transferred to the maternity hospital where I was given another u/s which showed baby in left tube and free fluid, I was rushed to surgery within 2 hours where my left tube and baby were removed, I had lost 1.5 liters of blood and needed 2 blood transfusions, when I came around although I was lucky to be alive I didn't care and I just remember a total feeling of emptiness and was crying all the time.

I was released from hospital 3 days later and battled with depression for a few months after but thankfully I managed to come out of that dark place and am slowly getting on with life although it can be very hard sometimes

I miss my 2 angels Bella & Bubs so much, I am not ready to even think about trying again at the moment although I was given the all clear as my HSG test showed no blockage in my right tube which is good news.

Anonymous

I had a miscarriage a few years ago and had lots of problems afterwards. I kept having pain and bleeding but the docs said it was nothing to worry about. After a few weeks of this and several visits to the doc and hospital they eventually decided to do an exploratory op with a camera. They found an ectopic pregnancy and had to have my tube removed, turns out I had been pregnant with twins and they had separated. The ectopic was nearly 12 weeks!! Thought I would share this.

Anonymous

I'm 22 years old and from UK. I had an ectopic when I was 19. I didn't no I was pregnant; I was bleeding for a few days but thought it was just my normal period. One morning I woke up in horrific pain down my left side. That afternoon a doctor came out to see me and gave me tablets as they thought it was my bowels. Anyways that same night the pain became unbearable, another doctor came out n said I needed to go to hospital. They thought it was my appendix. Blood tests were taken n that's when I was told I was pregnant. I never have been so shocked. More tests were taken to try find out why I was getting the pain I was. Then I was told I was having an ectopic. I hadn't even heard of that before. I just wasn't grasping what I was getting told. All I knew was I was too be having an operation the next day. Wasn't till then it hit me. Just found out I'm pregnant, but was soon too be taken away from me. That was it all over. Till this day, I cry like it only happened yesterday. I don't always no how to cope with losing my child. I was 5 weeks when it all happened and I just can't get my head around it all. It's been nearly 4 year in September and it's still killing me inside. I have gone on to having 2 children, a boy and a girl. 3 month after my ectopic, I got pregnant. Everyone's different. I'm blessed for the children I have. I still get pain down my left side; my left tube was removed during the op. So sorry for long post, but I've kept this pain to If for this long.

Anonymous

I had an ectopic back in March, a month before my 27th birthday; it was my third failed

pregnancy. After suffering a Molar, and a missed miscarriage, I had done so much research and

never thought I'd suffer an ectopic, I read so many horror stories about them. I

ended up getting pregnant about two weeks after my second lose; I was excited it

happened so quickly because I so badly wanted a baby. I started bleeding and had some

slight pain, I went to the ER and after a day full of test and ultrasounds they

determined I was having another Molar, I was devastated. I had the D&C a day or two

later. After about two days I got a call saying there was no baby in the tissue taken

from the D&C. So hurried back to get my blood checked, my levels were still rising so

they determined then that it was ectopic. I had to make the decision of surgery or the

shot, I chose the shot, went and got it, about two hours later of resting at home the

pain was unbearable, I rushed back to the hospital, and ended up getting emergency

surgery at about 1am. My right fallopian tube had ruptured and could not be saved.

They were all very apologetic, and claimed that due to my extremely high pain

tolerances they didn't realize it was beyond anything the shot could of done. I

wasn't very pleased. I can try again in September. To be honest the thought of being

pregnant again and losing another baby scares me. But I will have one someday. And it

will all be so worth it♡ thanks for letting me share my story.

 -Emily

My name is Cailey and I'm 23 years old. Me and my husband got married when I was 17. After

trying to conceive for a year, I finally got a positive pregnancy test! Everything was perfect until

my first ultrasound at 16 weeks. We found out our son had a fatal birth defect called anencephaly.

He was stillborn at 21 weeks. We were devastated and terrified to have another baby and

possibly lose it. But we were lucky to have two rainbow babies! A boy a year after losing our son

and a girl 19 months after that! We decided that we were done having children after our daughter

was born premature so during my c-section I had a tubal legation. People always asked why I got

my tubes tied at such a young age (I was 21). Part of it was because I really only wanted two

children but the biggest part was that I didn't want to worry about losing another baby ever again.

I thought a tubal was the only way to be sure of that. That was the worst decision of my life. I

ended up suffering from post tubal ligation syndrome. I lost hair; breast mass and I couldn't keep

any weight on. The worst part was the pain I had every month and the hormone imbalance that

made me insane. I thought I would live with that forever but almost two years after my tubal, I

missed a period. I was shocked to find out I was pregnant! I knew that it was likely to be ectopic

so at the first sign of pain I rushed to the ER. They did an ultrasound and to our amazement there

was an gestational sac in my uterus! There wasn't an fetal pole but they said I was too early to

see it. I was excited and scared but happy that it wasn't ectopic. But I started bleeding and

cramping. The doctor said it was a blighted ovum. It was depressing to think that my baby beat

the odds of implanting correctly just to not form right. I took medicine to cause me to miscarry.

When my hcg levels didn't go down they did another ultrasound. They didn't see anything and

decided to send me to a doctor with better equipment. As soon as the new doctor looked he saw

the ectopic pregnancy. He said the sac in my uterus was a pseudo sac. I thought this was some cruel trick of nature. After discussing all the options we decided to remove both of my tubes so it wouldn't happen again. I was crushed. But there was a silver lining. My post tubal legation syndrome is completely gone!

Cailey

In April of 2013 I started dating and fell in love with my now husband. We were so happy & so in love, we got a house together (rented it) in august and found out September 21 that we were expecting. At work on September 23 I started having light cramps on my right lower abdominal. I kind of blew it off as the cramping everyone feels when everything is attaching and going into place. On Oct 1 I got up for work and while brushing my teeth I doubled over in pain. I was crying it hurt so bad. I called into work and Dillen tried, but they said he could be fires if he missed. He went to work and I went to the ER. After blood work, urine test & a vaginal ultrasound they decided I had a cyst in my right ovary and sent me home. On Oct 4 I seen my Dr & told her what was going on. We did blood work and looked at my hcg levels. They hadn't doubled. On the 5th I was back in the ER. Again levels went up but barely. And they did another vaginal ultrasound. When I went to the Dr again on the 7th & checked my levels but they barely moved. She said there was no doubt in her mind it was a tubal pregnancy and I needed to do the methotrexate shot.

I was in and out of the hospital after that, couldn't go in public (every time I saw a baby I'd lose it) and even though Dillen was right next to me every step of the way (work all night & Dr offices all day) our happy go lucky relationship changed.

My emotions were everywhere. I'd cry over everything and get so mad I'd yell and throw stuff. I tried kicking him out, he wouldn't leave, I tried leaving, he wouldn't let me etc. All of this went on til January when I finally talked to a friend about it and she had miscarriage years before and gave me 2 books that helped her. They sat on my shelf for almost 2 months. We bought a house in Feb and got married in April. We fought on our due date (May 26) and found out we were preg on

May 31. Levels went up, didn't double and started dropping June 12, we lost our 2nd baby.

I cry everyday. Dillen Cry's often, when he thinks I'm asleep. But truth is... I don't sleep. I barely

eat. We don't fight as much now. I am finding other ways to release my emotions. I'm realizing

that even though we lost our babies we still have each other and of we keep fighting g we will

lose that too and that's not something either of us can handle.

I have dreams about my babies...I also have nightmares. I cry for them in my sleep, I cry when

I'm awake. This story doesn't have a happy ending. There are no sunshine & rainbows for us...

Yet. One day we will have a child, we might birth it or we might adopt it. Or maybe both. But , we

have each other. And I know my angels are with my great grandma, my papa, my grandpa & my

brother in law.... They are being taken care of and I know I will hold them one day. Until then I

hold them in my heart!

Anonymous

My story began when I returned from visiting my now ex-boyfriend who was in the army and getting out. I had returned the end of April and found out I was expecting just shortly after. I had just told my dad that I was pregnant and then I stood up to go to the bathroom and I collapsed in my mom's hallway and hit my head. She called 9-1-1 and was taken to the hospital where I passed out not once but twice and hit my head once. They did the two ultra sounds to see what was making me black out and they seen that I had a ruptured tube and a lot of blood in my stomach. They were not sure how much till I got back in surgery. Because of the doctors fast actions I am still here today. If they emergency department did not care about there jobs or there patients I would not be here to tell my story that happened on may 4th 2013. It has been a long hard year and I do find myself crying when I thing what she may look like. I do not know for a fact if it was a girl or a boy but I have a feeling it was a girl... I was only 5 weeks or so. After the procedure I went through a really tough time. I was depressed and didn't want to live. I had a friend that went through one a few years prior and she is the one who helped me the most since he didn't want to talk to me. Just say it got so bad that I took the pain meds the doctor gave me and I had an out of body experience and well just say if stopped after that. Then only three weeks after I lost her I went for my check up and she said wow this is pretty fast for someone to heal, and released me to go to everyday work.

I am terrified that I will have another ectopic pregnancy and never be to hold my own child. May we all stick together during out tough times!

Anonymous

Hi, my first ectopic was 3 years ago this month. My husband and I were trying for 18 months and when we finally got the 2 lines we were ecstatic to say the least.

A week later I started spotting brown colored discharge and went to a&e they mentioned it could be an ectopic, so booked in for a scan the next day but they couldn't see anything so we had blood taken and went back 48 hours later for another lot of blood, it rose but didn't rise enough so they took more blood and repeated the process then scanned me again and found the baby growing outside the ovary on my left side. The doctors said it was too far gone to use methotrexate and I would have surgery the next day to remove the tube. Then the next day as I was being pushed down the surgery a medical junior said I was able to have the drug as I was borderline. So I opted to have the injection. A few days later I went back for bloods but my hormones were not dropping so I have another dose, they sent me home and that night 30-7-2011 my tube ruptured. I phoned an ambulance who came round quite quickly, I told the paramedics what was happening but they seemed to think I was constipated. After demanding they take me to hospital, I was left in a&e without pain relief from 12am until 6am when they finally found my notes and took me to the gynecology ward. Where I has an internal exam, and given morphine and anti sickness drugs. I can still taste the sick and smell it now. Like rotten eggs.

At 11am I finally went for a scan and as soon as the lady inserted the Doppler into me her reaction was " oh my god it's ruptured you need surgery now" then I was rushed to theatre at 1pm and outside before being out to sleep the surgeon came through and said " what side is your ectopic because we can't locate your notes" I said the left. Then I woke up on the ward later that day and discharged the next. I will never forgive the hospital for making me of through all that when it could have been dealt with a lot faster. I had a second ectopic May of 2012 but opted to have mtx before I lost my remaining tube. Today I found I am pregnant, I don't know whether I am imagining pains in my right side or not. I have to wait for an emergency scan next week. The waiting game begins again.

Anonymous

Two months after a camping trip, I wasn't feeling well. My mother suggested I could be pregnant. I took a test and it was positive! My husband and I were happy and scared at the same time. This baby would be our 3rd child and we weren't that young at 28 years old. After time, the pain progressed. I kept trying to ignore it and stay positive by talking about names: Xavier, Gabriella, Malachi, and Seth with my husband, but deep down I knew something wasn't right. One day, our electric went out (there was a wide spread outage), so we went to stay at my grandfathers. Eventually the pain got so intense; I decided to go to the local ER. The local ER only ran a pregnancy test, released me, and told me to get a check up at the doctor. I went the next day to the doctor they suggested and they wouldn't see me for 2 weeks, even though I could barely walk from the pain. I told my husband that I was dying that day and basically said my goodbyes. My best friend told me to call her OB/GYN. I did and got an appointment the next day. The doctor was trying to keep us positive but I knew what was coming. We went into the ultrasound room and there wasn't a heart beat. She couldn't find the baby. After what seems like an eternity, the doctor came in and started talking about ectopic pregnancies. She told me to go straight to the ER that she would call and let them know I was on my way. I made it out of the building and into my vehicle before I started crying while feeling like they were going to kill my child. I wasn't thinking clearly, of course. After I calmed down, I checked into the ER, where hours of testing and ultrasounds were performed on me. Finally the ER OB/GYN told me I had to be rushed into Emergency surgery. I still thought I was dying and said my goodbyes. I prayed for my husband and children to have a great life without me. Next thing I know, I was waking up from surgery. The nurse asked me if I was awake and I immediately asked where are my husband and mom? They then came back to be with me in recovery and I spent the day, night, and next morning in the hospital. The ER OB/GYN told us that my Fallopian tube had burst and was leaking into my stomach. If I wouldn't have came to the Dr/ER, I would have died. I was put on the floor with new mothers, in which I felt was like a cruel joke because I was asked by all the nurses if I had a girl or boy. I told my night nurse, I wanted to get up as soon possible. I didn't tell anyone, but all I wanted to do was crawl in my bed at home and cry. July 3rd, 2012, I gained an angel. This year makes 2 years since the miscarriage but the memories are fresh in my mind. I can only hope I see my angel baby one day and that he or she is as beautiful as I imagine.

Anonymous

I had a cervical ectopic pregnancy. On March 17th, I took a pregnancy test. It immediately turned positive! I was so happy! I quit smoking immediately and changed my eating habits. I called my doctor to set up an appointment. About a week later, while at work, I felt a little fluid but didn't think anything of it. But a few minutes later, I felt it again. I went into the bathroom and I saw bright red blood. I immediately called my husband and told him. He said he was on his way. I then called my dad and asked him to bring me to the hospital. He also said he would be there in a minute. Within 5 minutes, the ambulance was there. My husband called them. They took me to the hospital. I laid there bleeding for hours. I was getting upset. My mom went out to find a nurse. I had to use the bathroom but I was not able to get up on my own because I was feeling dizzy. They came in and unhooked me and on the way to the bathroom, my husband complained about the amount of time that we were there and not once had anyone been in to see me. The nurse replied that they had real medical emergencies that had to be dealt with. A few hours later, shift change happened. The new nurse came in and asked how I was doing. We told her that we have been there for 7 hours and not once was I seen. She asked me if I went for my ultrasound. When I told her no, she went out and screamed at everyone there...within 15 minutes, I was on my way for my ultrasound. The sonogram tech tried an abdominal ultrasound but couldn't see anything so he did a transvaginal ultrasound still nothing. He said chances are that it was just way too early to see anything. I got back to my room and the doctor came in and told me that my HCG level was quite high so they knew I was pregnant. She released me and told me to follow up with my doctor. We called the next day and they had me come in. They checked my hcg levels every other day and also did a sonogram every other day....still nothing but the HCG level was still climbing. On March 29th, they noticed a huge blood vessel on my tube. It was so big, that my doctor thought I was having a tubal pregnancy. He decided that I needed to go to the OR because he was concerned that the tube was going to rupture. I woke up from surgery to be told that the baby wasn't in my tubes and I was still pregnant! I was so happy!! I went home that evening. I was sore from the incisions but very happy. I went back the next day for a check up and my doctor mentioned giving me a shot to terminate. I refused. My baby wasn't in the tubes. I was still thinking that it was an early pregnancy and it would show up eventually. I went the weekend with no issues. But Monday morning I woke up to bleeding very heavily. I called the doctor and they said to go down right away. I was taken in immediately. They had me leave a urine sample and then put me in for the ultrasound. They started and still nothing. My mom was with me. We were both discouraged. All of a sudden, we heard a heartbeat! I looked at the screen and there was my sweet baby! Heart was just beating away and those little movements! My mom and I both started laughing and crying tears of joy. But that moment lasted 30 seconds. The ultrasound tech said Tina, the baby isn't going to make it, it has implanted on your cervix. My mom's tears of joy became tears of sorrow. I told her that the sonogram tech was wrong. I told her that we see the baby and she was fine. I asked her to call my husband and dad and tell them the wonderful news. She said that we needed to wait. I said no, I asked for the phone and called my dad. I told him that we got to see the baby and she was perfect. My mom asked to talk to my dad. I handed her the phone and she was telling him to get my husband and get to the hospital right away. I was yelling that there was no need to, that my baby was ok. While she was talking, I looked down and there was blood everywhere. I started begging god to please let my baby be ok . My doctor came in and explained that I had to go to the OR to remove the pregnancy. He said that I was bleeding out and that I was in danger. I asked him to put my baby where she belonged. He said they couldn't. That once they detach the baby, the baby would be gone in seconds. I begged him to please not kill my baby. He kept apologizing but said there was nothing they could do. This was an emergency and I was at a risk of having a hysterectomy or losing my life. They put me in a wheelchair and literally ran me over to the main part of the hospital to be prepped. My dad, husband, and sister came in and hugged me. When my dad got to me, I hugged him and said "daddy, please don't let them kill my baby, please daddy please". He told me that he was sorry but I was going to die if I didn't do this. I got into the OR and my doctor yelled at me. He said if I let him do his job 3 days prior, that this wouldn't be happening. I apologized and completely lost it. He apologized to me. The anesthesiologist, put the mask on me and was putting pressure on my artery in my neck and was talking about "cool icebergs"...I was still begging them not to do this and I would not go to sleep. The next thing I knew, I was in the recovery room. I started screaming. The heartbreak was unimaginable. They had my entire family come into recovery room to try and console me. They called up to L&D and had a grief counselor come and talk to me. She held me, rubbed my head, kissed me and cried with me. She told me about her loss. She gave me her number and told me to call her anytime. I was released a while later. This was April 2, 2007

Tina Marie Bushey-Ruger

Here is my story I already have 2 children but we were driving to Nevada and I was feeling sick so after we got to Vegas and got unpacked I went and got a test a few days later because I was still sick. The test came back positive and we were shocked and happy I thought I couldn't have any more. I set up an appointment to go to the doctors but I started spotting a few days later. The sporting only started to get worse and I started to feel light headed and dizzy like I was going to pass out, followed by my stomach hurting. My husband took me to UMC emergency room and they checked me and did an ultrasound. They said they couldn't see anything in my uterus but that it might be because I was so early pregnant. They told me to come back two days later for blood work to see if my hormones were rising. I went home and they next day we went to Wal-Mart I picked my son up and I felt something pull it was the worst pain I have ever felt I started bleeding a little more than I had been so we went home then pain didn't stop so we called an ambulance they took me back to the hospital and put me in a is option room because they said I also had adult chickenpox surprise for me. They did a other ultrasound and saw baby was in my left tube and I was hemorrhaging so the took me for emergency surgery all the while I was crying so hard for my baby I wanted so badly they took out my baby and my left tube I was 14 weeks along. I went home the next day with an empty feeling I never found out if it was a boy or a girl I always wonder and it hurts to not know. A year after my ectpic I found out I was pregnant again I worried if it would be ectpic and I was amazed I was pregnant again because one tube it's harder to get pregnant. The baby was just fine and I had a little boy October 30th 2014. I like to feel it was my baby wasn't ready to be born when I had the ectopic but he was ready a year later when my Austin was born like he came back. There is hope after an ectopic pregnancy, for another healthy baby never give up hope. You can use my picture if you want to publish my story and my name Regina Kendall.

Regina Kendall

On November 9th, 2013 I went to the hospital at 3 months pregnant and found out I had a miscarriage I healed okay and then April 4th, 2014 I went to The Florida Hospital - Apopka Branch in em-bearable pain in my lower abdomen. Had no idea I was pregnant after waiting 2 hours in the E.R. they took some blood and told me they were going to do an ultrasound and wanted to make sure it wasn't an ectopic pregnancy I said I didn't even know I was pregnant. (Apparently they forgot to tell me that I was pregnant when they did the urine sample) so after 4 hours of waiting in the E.R. they finally got an ultrasound done and came back after 2 more hours and told me they were going to transport me to The Florida Hospital - Orlando South Branch and that I was probably having an ectopic pregnancy so they transferred me about 2 hours after that and then when I got to the hospital they had no room for me so I am still in unbearable pain and still confused cause I didn't even know i was pregnant they had to take my left tube and ovary I really want 3 more children but they said that if i ever get pregnant again to immediately go to the hospital I had a 6 week old baby growing in my tube

P.S. I really like your page y'all are very helpful when I get depressed

Samantha Smith

I was having bad cramping for a few weeks and light bleeding to moderate bleeding. I finally said hey this isn't right... I made a doc appointment it was March 14th 2014 when I went into my appt they ran a pregnancy test and told me I was pregnant. I was full with joy fear happiness and all mixed emotions. I had an appointment with our family doc for an ultrasound and blood work that following Monday. I have an almost 2 year old (7.20.12) that I told her that Friday night that I had a baby in my belly. She kept saying baby and rubbing my belly. Well Saturday night I was bleeding very heavily so went to the ER.. They diagnosed me with a threatened miscarriage and sent me home. They told me to see my doc Monday for an ultrasound. So I email my doc he wanted me to wait because my hormones were still raising. All Friday sat and sun night I kept telling my boyfriend I don't know what I'll do if I loose our baby... Well come Monday I had my Labs and then about an hour and a half after I totally want down hill. I went to the bathroom and when I went to stand up I fell to the ground I was very dizzy and kept blacking out. I called my mom to ask her to take my daughter because I was sick and told her to hurry. She asked what was wrong I told her that I'd talk to her when she got to my house. We'll when she got there I couldn't stand I couldn't walk, craw,l nothing. I told her I was pregnant and that something is very wrong. She then called the ambulance. I had to have the 2 cops help me up and then a wheel chair down the stairs then to the ambulance bed. On the way he asked me if my shoulder hurt I told him yes he said he was going to diagnose me with ectopic pregnancy... I was scared I told him I didn't want to loose my baby that I was very scared. I got to the hospital I need an IV and I needed blood. I was so dehydrated and had such a blood loss they couldn't find my veins. I was then transferred by helicopter to abbot in Saint Paul because I needed emergency surgery. I kept telling the surgeon and pleading her to save my baby. Well that was not the case she just kept telling me she was very sorry. And that it was time for surgery. We went to the OR and the last thing I remember was them putting me on a very cold table. After that they were trying to wake me up in the recovery room. I'm still very crushed. It turns out I had over a liter and a half if blood in my stomach and that my fallopian tube had burst. They were able to save my tubes and surgery went well I was in the hospital for 3 days. I was not able to take care of my daughter for about a month so my mom had her. It really took a toll on me because when we got home from the hospital my boyfriend was there for me but when he had to go back to work he was out of town I felt like I didn't just loose my baby angel but my family too. I still get very depressed and wonder what I've done still scared to have sex sometimes and I'm scared to get pregnant again because I don't know if I could do it again... .. I'm just reaching out to these ectopic pregnancy support sites.

Anonymous

Hey here's my story...

I woke up with pains on my right side.. I had been bleeding for a few days so just assumed I was on my period! I did however take a test around 530pm that day which came back as positive! I then rung up my local clinic but they couldn't give me any advice over the phone and they told me to ring 111 which I did when speaking to them at 111 they wanted me to go to my local doctors for an evaluation, when I went to the doctors I was then told I had to go to the hospital as it could be an ectopic pregnancy. I got there around 9pm had to wait around an hour and a half to be seen.. They took 3 lots of blood, put a catheter in my hand and I was told I'd have to stay in overnight!

My blood pressure was checked numerous times during the night! In the morning I went down to have an internal examination and they said there was a mass on my right side. At first I was told I would need surgery which scared the heck out of me! But they then informed me that I could have the methotrexate injection. I got given that 3 days after I was admitted. I had awful stomach cramps for days and had been bleeding non stop. I was admitted on 9th June and I'm still bleeding but my hormone levels have now gone down to 40 so they're hopeful that they will be at a negative next week. I feel that although I was unlucky to have this happen to me it's also made me more aware of how much worse my situation could have been.

Thanks for reading

My story..... i had my ectopic last year in February.... I was bleeding round middle of January I thought I was early coming on after a week a week I was still bleeding so went to doctors done a wee sample I had white blood cells so gave me a 3 day course.... I didn't take the tablets I brought a test with in seconds it came up straight away I rang my doctors who told me to go straight to a&e as it sounded like a miscarriage this was Tuesday 29th I was at a&e got seen doctor felt round my tummy I was in pain in my lower area I was told to go home let nature take its course... I waited a week which felt like a lifetime to do another test it came up positive on Wednesday I went back to my doctors and was booked in early stages clinic for a scan for 18th February.... I tried to take it easy but in Thursday 30th I left work in agonizing pain I went home just lay down... Friday I was ok.... on Saturday I was back in pain I was sent to a&e where they sent me to early stages for an internal I had my bloods taken and still showing infection but my cervix was closed so I was told ectopic was ruled out and it could be a threatening miscarriage... as my pain was my right side... I went home took tablets they gave me on Tuesday I went back into hospital in to much pain with high fever and was told it could be gallstone, appendix, water infection I was told I wasn't having a miscarriage my temperature was to high... I was given antibiotics and overnight stay I still wasn't scanned.... my appointment finally arrived it was time for my scan I had scan and internal was told I miscarriage.... They took my bloods and wee sample it still came up positive... my hormone level was over 7000.... So I had more bloods done and it dropped a little... A doctor decided was to look inside through the belly button to see what it was I went to threate at 5.30pm on Monday 18th Feb 2013 I didn't wake up till Tuesday 19th at 2pm I ended up intensive care on life support as during surgery I vomited and my left lung collapsed.... I had an ectopic pregnancy I had my right tube partly removed and my ectopic was 8cm..... I was given 4 weeks off work to recover.... I gutted because I was told I've had one I'm more likely to have another I pray and hope that isn't the case.... I've had an emotional roller coaster ride all because they didn't scan me straight away. ...Some months I don't get periods I take a test and negative then month later in come on....

Anonymous

My story:

Me and husband were married 2 short months when we found out we were pregnant. September 5th 2010, a day I know I will never forget! We were all excited telling the whole family, but that very same day I had went to the bathroom and noticed I was spotting, I thought maybe it was implantation bleeding so I didn't think about it anymore. After a couple of days past I started bleeding worse so I went to my obgyn and he did blood test.

  He gave me the worst news my heart could ever bare, I was having an eptopic pregnancy I didn't want to believe him. So the next couple of days it was every other hour I was having blood drawn, and more and more! I couldn't stand it anymore so I found another Dr, and he did everything the other one did and told me it was just a bad pregnancy. He gave me an option to have a surgery to see where my baby was or to get a shot to terminate my pregnancy, automatically I denied the shot. On my way to the hospital I could feel something wasn't right I started feeling light headed, nauseated, ETC but I suffered through the paper work but by the time I got to the lab to get my paper work done I was in so much pain I couldn't stand it. As I walking out of the lab I just dropped to my knees luckily my husband grabbed me up ran to the car and flew to the emergency room where they were waiting on me with a wheel chair all I remember was a bunch of people stripping me of my clothes and wheeling me to emergency surgery. All in all I lost 3 pints of blood and an angel that I would have gladly given my life for as you can see on 9/21/10 I lost a part of me that I will never get back even though the Lord blessed me with a beautiful 4 month old daughter my heart will always rest with my angel baby! Thank you for given me the opportunity to share my story!

My baby's story

I was 18 and didn't know I was pregnant until the day before the worst day ever. I was staying with my parents that night and planning on taking a pregnancy test there. It didn't take but a second to find out it was positive. I was excited because I have always known I was meant to be a mom. The next morning when I woke up I seen that I was spotting but my mom reassured me that it can be normal to spot early in a pregnancy. I was going with my mom to a doctor's appointment 2 hours away so we got in the car and left. 1 hour into the trip I started hurting all over. I could barely breathe but I kept telling myself that everything was fine when it wasn't. Little did I know my life was slipping away and so was my baby's. On the way back home we stopped and I noticed I was no longer spotting I was bleeding heavily. I was in more pain than I have ever been in my life. I knew something was wrong but I didn't want to admit it. Finally I told my parents that I need to get to a hospital. We were almost home so they took me to our local emergency room. I was so scared but I remember sitting in the waiting room telling myself that everything was fine. I couldn't have been more wrong. When I got to the room they were waiting to take me to radiology for an internal ultrasound. I couldn't see my baby for too much blood. Before I got back to my room the doctor was waiting to tell me the worst news I have ever gotten. My baby was an ectopic pregnancy and my right fallopian tube had ruptured. I needed immediate surgery and there was no time to wait because I had already lost too much blood and I was dying. I said no. I begged her to let me go because I believed that if I went home I would be okay and my baby would be okay. I begged her to just let me leave. I started walking out the door and my parents showed up. That is when it all became real for me. I signed the paper and before I could get to the operating room I lost consciousness. I was dying and so was my baby. I didn't get a chance to hold my baby or tell it how much I loved it before someone was cutting it out of me and calling it medical waist. After surgery I had a dream that I was holding a baby girl. I know I don't know the sex of my baby but I believe God let me say hello and goodbye to my baby and it was a girl. Her name is Chasity Marie and my surgery was 7\11\07. It will be 7 years in less than two weeks and I have done nothing but think about my baby lately. I have a 1 year old daughter now and I tell her that she is baby sister. I hope my baby in heaven knows it can never be forgotten or replaced. I write her letters and get her gifts every year on July 11th and I keep them in a treasure box. Please share my story. Please put it in your book. All I have of my baby is our story and this may be the only was I can share my baby with the world. You may use my name. I am not ashamed of my baby or what happened.

Brittany Farmer

Hello, your page outs such an inspiration to me. I had my first ectopic in November of 09. I'd already had 1 1/2 yr old son. I'd just gotten married in October of 08. Losing my Angel was the worst experience. I found out I was pregnant at the E.R. I'd been really campy. After the ultrasound they found I was indeed 4 wks pregnant. They saw no sac & my levels were low & they found the baby was in my right fallopian tube. They gave me methotrexate to dissolve the pregnancy... some of the worst pain I've ever had to endure. I shed so many tears. The metho was successful. I had to stand by & feel my baby die inside me. I did a lot of praying I felt like although I had my husband who was there, all I really had was God, only he knew my pain.

In Jan. 2011 I successfully had another beautiful baby boy. In Jan. 2013 I surprisingly found out I was once again pregnant via home pregnancy test. I was ecstatic. I went to the E.R. once again because I couldn't get an earlier appointment and I really wanted to know something... after the ultrasound I found out it was once again an ectopic, in the exact same tube. They treated me with metho again. I went back the next 2 days and everything looked normal my levels we're reacting to the meds progressively... a few days later I had the worst pain, I was rushed to have emergency surgery because my tube had ruptured. I thank God for my husband being my support system. He truly took care of me. He never left my side while in the hospital... after all of that. My tube had to be removed. My DR said, it would be hard for me to conceive again because my left tube could be damaged as well. I gave up trying I had God, my 2 boys and an awesome husband. I had a dream during my recovery that I was on the phone with my dr & he kept saying you're 6wks pregnant but in the dream I said how is that possible? Lol 6 months later, I was pregnant with my now 4 month old son. All things are possible, even through all that pain. God would never leave you & when we trust him, he'll make what the Enemy meant for our bad, for our good! God bless you, I pray that you'll be encouraged.

Kelly Hutson

After Cindy lost her baby to Ruptured Ectopic Pregnancy December 12, 2005, she has been researching about Ectopic Pregnancies and has been steadily active in the baby loss community. She has since decided to gather stories from women all over the world to put into one book to hopefully be able to reach families all over the world to give them hope and let them know they are not alone. Cindy offers support on her Facebook pages to families and is working hard in her community to offer support and hope to everyone she meets.

Lightning Source UK Ltd.
Milton Keynes UK
UKOW02f1912140515

251552UK00001B/127/P